ADVICE TO MOTHERS.

ADVICE TO MOTHERS

ON THE

MANAGEMENT OF THEIR OFFSPRING.

BY

PYE HENRY CHAVASSE,

MEMBER OF THE ROYAL COLLEGE OF SURGEONS, LONDON.

LONDON:
LONGMAN, ORME, BROWN, GREEN, & LONGMANS.
BARLOW, BIRMINGHAM.

M.DCCC.XXXIX.

BIRMINGHAM:
PRINTED BY J. C. BARLOW, BENNETT'S HILL.

TO

JOSEPH HODGSON, Esq., F.R.S.,

&c., &c.,

𝔈𝔥𝔦𝔰 𝔚𝔬𝔯𝔨 𝔦𝔰 𝔇𝔢𝔡𝔦𝔠𝔞𝔱𝔢𝔡,

IN TESTIMONY OF THE RESPECT AND ESTEEM

OF

THE AUTHOR.

PREFACE.

It has fallen to my lot to witness the prejudices and mistakes, and consequent dangers, which mothers, especially young ones, fall into, from the want of some little work to guide them in the management of their offspring.

When it is considered that the first years—nay, months—of an infant's life frequently determine whether he shall live, or (if he live) whether he shall be healthy or otherwise, it would appear that too much attention cannot be paid to the subject.

Several works have been written on the management of children, but none, I conceive, have been sufficiently explicit, or have entered enough into minutiæ, or have dwelt on that which is of as much or more importance than the cure of disease, namely, the prevention.

As none other more competent person has filled up (what appears to me) this vacuum, I have ventured to send forth the few following hints.

I have not broached any new doctrines, nor made any new discoveries. All that I have attempted is, to have written useful advice, in a clear style, stripped of all technicalities, which mothers of every station may understand.

It may be said I have descended too much into particulars, and that I have dilated upon subjects not strictly coming under the province of a medical man. But, with due deference, I reply that nothing is too trivial that will tend to preserve health; that a medical man should not only be acquainted with *all things* that may conduce to it, but, at the same time, communicate that knowledge to others; that he should not only be able to cure disease, but, as far as in him lies, prevent it. The remarks I have made have all, I trust, conspired to this end.

I have adopted a conversational form, as being more familiar, and as an easier method of making myself understood.

An impartial public will determine how far I have performed my task satisfactorily.

BIRMINGHAM,
    12, OLD SQUARE.

CONTENTS.

Part I.—INFANCY.

	PAGE.	QUES.
On Ablution.		
The temperature of the water a new-born infant is washed with	21	1
The practice of washing a new-born infant's head with brandy	22	2
General observations on the washing of a new-born infant	22	3
On the Management of the Navel String.		
The period of time the navel-string separates from the body	24	5
Remarks on the separation of the navel-string	24	6
Treatment of a sore navel	24	7
On Clothing.		
Flannel caps for new-born infants	25	8

CONTENTS.

	PAGE.	QUES.
Best kind of belly-band	25	9
Remarks on the clothing of an infant	25	10
Observations on the airing of an infant's clothes	26	11
Caps for infants	26	12

On Diet.

	PAGE.	QUES.
The period of time after birth at which an infant should be put to the breast	27	13
The plan to be adopted when a mother has no milk *immediately* after her confinement	28	14
The stated periods to be observed in suckling	29	15
Remarks on the giving of food to infants	29	16
The best substitute for a mother's milk	29	17
The stated periods to be observed in giving an infant at the breast artificial food	31	18
Advice to mothers unable to suckle their infants	31	19
Observations on the choosing of a wet nurse	33	20
Diet of a wet nurse	34	21
Further hints on the management of a wet nurse	36	22
The proper age for weaning an infant	37	23
The weaning of an infant	38	24
The diet of a weaned infant	38	25
Remarks on the addition of gin or peppermint to infants' food	38	26
On sugar for sweetening infants' food	39	27

	PAGE.	QUES.

On Vaccination.

	PAGE.	QUES.
The great value of vaccination	40	28
The good effects of vaccination, even in those rare cases of smallpox after vaccination	40	29
The great importance of re-vaccination	41	30
Observations on the communication of other diseases at the time of vaccination	41	31
The age at which an infant should be vaccinated	41	32
Under what circumstances vaccination should be deferred	42	33
Remarks on the administration of medicine after vaccination	42	34

On Dentition.

	PAGE.	QUES.
The time at which dentition commences	42	35
The number of the first set of teeth, and the usual order in which they appear	43	36
Observations on the lancing of an infant's gums	44	37
Remarks on the hardening of infants' gums after lancing them	44	38
The treatment of convulsions from teething	44	39
The best gum-sticks for infants	45	40
Fruit during dentition	45	41
The prevention of diseases induced by dentition	46	42
Remarks on the administration of absorbents, to restrain purging, during teething	47	43

CONTENTS.

	PAGE.	QUES.
Observations on cough medicines to relieve "tooth cough"	48	44
The danger of healing eruptions behind the ears from teething	48	45

ON EXERCISE.

	PAGE.	QUES.
How soon after birth an infant may be taken into the air	49	46
Injurious effects of *violent* tossing of new-born infants	50	47

ON SLEEP.

	PAGE.	QUES.
The temperature of an infant's sleeping apartment	50	48
Remarks on an infant sleeping alone	51	49
The *rocking* an infant to sleep	51	50
Hints on the covering of the head of the crib	51	51
The importance of a great deal of sleep for an infant	52	52
The reason why much sleep is so beneficial	53	53
The practice of giving composing medicines to infants reprobated	53	54

ON AILMENTS, &c.

	PAGE.	QUES.
Collection of mucus in the air-passages of new-born infants	54	55
The best medicine for a new-born infant	54	56
The distinction between slight and serious diseases	54	57
The cause and treatment of chafing	55	58

	PAGE.	QUES.
The best remedies for costiveness of infants	56	59
Means for preventing the costiveness of infants	57	60
The causes and remedies for flatulence	57	61
The cause and treatment of hickup	59	62
The cause and remedies for looseness of the bowels	59	63
The symptoms and treatment of red gum	60	64
The means of preventing and curing "snuffles"	60	65
Remarks on the sickness of infants	61	66
Causes, symptoms, prevention, and cure of thrush	62	67
Remarks on beef-tea and broths for delicate infants at the breast	64	68
Means to restrain immoderate bleeding from leech-bites	64	69
Advice to a mother on her own management during the illness of her infant	65	70

Part II.—CHILDHOOD.

On Ablution.

	PAGE.	QUES.
Hints on the washing of a child	69	71
The propriety of a child standing *in the water* considered	69	72
Remarks on the liability of producing cold and weakening the sight by washing a child's head	70	73

	PAGE.	QUES.
Remarks on the necessity of putting a child in his tub night and morning	70	74
The proper heat of the *body* when the child is placed in his tub	70	75
The best temperature of the water a child of a year old is washed in	71	76
The means of strengthening a delicate child	71	77
Friction after ablution	71	78

ON CLOTHING.

	PAGE.	QUES.
Remarks on the clothing of a child	72	79
The parts of the body, in particular, that should be kept warm	72	80
Flannel night-gowns	72	81
Observations on the hardening of children by light clothing	73	82
Flannel shirts for delicate children considered	73	83

ON DIET.

	PAGE.	QUES.
The diet of a child of a year old	74	84
The propriety of a child of a year and a half old having meat considered	74	85
Puddings for children	75	86
The breakfast of a child who has cut his teeth	75	87
The dinner of a child who has cut his teeth	75	88
Remarks on pork for a child	76	89
Remarks on veal	76	90

CONTENTS.

	PAGE.	QUES.
Remarks on salt and boiled beef	76	91
The best dinner for a child when there is nothing on the table which he may eat with impunity	77	92
The wholesomeness of potatoes considered	77	93
Remarks on other vegetables for children	77	94
Remarks on a mother being too particular in dieting her child	77	95
The best beverage for a child's dinner	78	96
The supper of a child who has cut his teeth	79	97
Observations on giving a delicate child wine	79	98
On the importance of investigating the cause of the sudden loss of appetite of children	79	99
Remarks on tea for a child of four or five years old	80	100
Remarks on beer for a boy	80	101
Cakes and sweetmeats for children	80	102
The comparative wholesomeness of bakers' and home-made bread	81	103
The wholesomeness of carraway seeds or currants in bread or cakes considered	81	104
Butter for children	82	105

ON THE NURSERY.

	PAGE.	QUES.
Remarks on the *ventilation* of a nursery	82	106
Observations on the *light* of a nursery	83	107
Further hints conducive to the well-doing of a child	83	108
Carpets in nurseries considered	84	109

	PAGE.	QUES.
Observations on the stopping of a nursery chimney, to prevent draughts	85	110

ON EXERCISE.

Sending a child out before breakfast considered	85	111
Remarks on the early putting of a child on his feet to walk	86	112
On children's carriages	86	113
Observations on sending a child out *in wet weather*	86	114
The number of times a day a child, in fine weather, should be sent out	87	115
On the best exercise for a child in wet weather	87	116

ON AMUSEMENTS.

Remarks on the amusements of children	88	117

ON EDUCATION.

Infant schools	88	118

ON SLEEP.

The best mattress for a child	89	119
On a child sleeping in the day-time	90	120
The time a child should be put to bed in the evening	90	121
Observations on the importance of washing and dressing a child *as soon as he awakes*	91	122
Remarks on a child lying alone	91	123

CONTENTS.

	PAGE.	QUES.

ON SECOND DENTITION.
The commencement of second dentition, &c. ... 91 124

ON DISEASE, &c.
Precursory signs of water on the brain ... 92 125
Precursory symptoms of croup ... 93 126
How to distinguish "tooth cough" from the cough of inflammation of the lungs ... 94 127
How to reduce the *large* bowels of children ... 94 128
The best aperients for children ... 95 129
Enemas of broth for delicate children considered ... 95 130
Means of strengthening a delicate child ... 95 131
Remarks on sea-bathing for young children ... 96 132
The best method of administering medicine to a child ... 96 133
Observations on the rousing of a child from his sleep to give him his medicine ... 97 134
Remarks on parents disobeying medical men's orders ... 97 135
Remarks on the management of a sick-room ... 101 136
Precautions to prevent inflammation of the lungs ... 102 137
Advice with regard to the confinement of a child within doors, who is prone to inflammation of the lungs ... 102 138
Means of expanding and strengthening the chest of a child who is chicken-breasted or narrow-chested ... 103 139
Means of preventing a child from wetting his bed while asleep ... 104 140

CONTENTS.

	PAGE.	QUES.
Plan of preventing and curing chilblains	104	141
On the prevention of worms	105	142
On the prevention of rickets	106	143

ON WARM BATHS.

| The complaints for which warm baths are useful | 106 | 144 |
| The precautions and rules to be attended to in putting a child into a warm bath | 106 | 145 |

ON ACCIDENTS.

The best application for a cut finger	108	146
The best application for a bruise	108	147
The best means of extinguishing the clothes of children when they are on fire	109	148
The best immediate application for a scald or burn	109	149

PART III.—YOUTH.

ON ABLUTION.

Remarks on cold bathing	113	150
Observations on tepid bathing	114	151
Remarks on warm bathing	115	152
Observations on warm bathing producing cold	115	153

CONTENTS.

	PAGE.	QUES.
ON CLOTHING.		
On wearing of flannel next the skin	116	154
On flannel producing irritation of the skin	116	155
Remarks on the wearing of a prepared hair skin over the chest	116	156
Observations on youth's waistcoats	117	157
Remarks on shoes and stockings	117	158
On stays for girls	118	159
Remarks on stays strengthening the body	118	160
On the effect stays have on the figure	119	161
Remarks on female dress	120	162
ON DIET.		
The best breakfast for a youth	121	163
The necessity of meat for breakfast considered	122	164
The best dinner for a youth	122	165
Remarks on the wholesomeness of broths and soups	123	166
Observations on beer, as a beverage for youths	123	167
Observations on wine for youths	124	168
On tea, as a beverage	124	169
The best supper for youth	124	170
On taking refreshment between meals	125	171
Remarks on pocket money for boys	125	172
ON EXERCISE.		
The best exercise for a youth	126	173
Horse and poney exercise considered	126	174
Carriage exercise considered	126	175

CONTENTS.

	PAGE.	QUES.
The best time of the day for taking exercise	127	176
The importance of refraining from exercise *immediately* after a meal	127	177

ON AMUSEMENTS.

	PAGE.	QUES.
The most beneficial amusements for boys	127	178
Remarks on wind instruments	128	179
On amusements for girls	128	180
The reason why balls are such fruitful sources of coughs, colds, and consumption	129	181
Remarks on girls foregoing the pleasures of a ball	130	182
Observations on singing and on reading aloud	130	183

ON EDUCATION.

	PAGE.	QUES.
On the selection of a female boarding school	130	184

ON THE CHOICE OF A PROFESSION OR TRADE.

	PAGE.	QUES.
The best profession or trade for a delicate youth	131	185

ON SLEEP.

	PAGE.	QUES.
Remarks on sleep, &c.	132	186
The number of hours of sleep necessary for a youth	134	187

ON PREVENTION OF DISEASE, &c.

	PAGE.	QUES.
On the organ most likely to become affected in *precocious* individuals	135	188

CONTENTS.

	PAGE.	QUES.
On the means of warding off danger in such cases	135	189
On the general health of precocious youths	138	190
The habit of body most predisposed to scrofula	139	191
On the importance of attending to a slight spitting of blood	139	192
On the means to prevent spitting of blood from ending in consumption	140	193
Precautions to prevent sore throat	142	194
Remarks on calomel as a purgative medicine, and on the best aperients for youth	142	195
The diseases peculiar to females	144	196
The usual causes of chlorosis	144	197
The symptoms of chlorosis	144	198
The prevention of chlorosis	145	199
The treatment of chlorosis	146	200
The symptoms of hysterics	146	201
The causes of hysterics	147	202
The prevention and cure of hysterics	147	203

CONCLUSION.

PART I.—INFANCY.

ADVICE TO MOTHERS.

PART I.—INFANCY

ABLUTION.

1.—*Question.* Is a new-born infant to be washed, for the first time, in *warm* or *cold* water?

Answer. It is not an uncommon plan to use *cold* water from the first, under the impression of its strengthening the child. This appears to be a cruel and barbarous practice, and likely to have a contrary tendency. Moreover, it frequently produces inflammation of the eyes, stuffing of the nose (snuffles), or looseness of the bowels. Although I do not approve of *cold* water, we must not run into an opposite extreme, as *hot* water would weaken and enervate the infant, and thus would predispose him to disease. Lukewarm *rain* water will be the best to wash him with. This, if it be summer, may have its temperature gradually lowered, until it be quite cold: if it be winter, a dash of warm water may still be added, to take off the chill.

2.—*Q.* Is it necessary to wash a new-born infant's head with brandy, to prevent him from taking cold?

A. It is not necessary. The idea that it will prevent cold is erroneous, as the rapid evaporation of heat, which the brandy causes, is more likely to give cold than otherwise.

3.—*Q.* Have you any general observations to make on the washing of a new-born infant?

A. A child should be thoroughly washed every morning, from head to foot; wetting the head first, and paying particular attention to the groin, hams, arm-pits, &c. The skin should be thoroughly dried after every ablution, and all the parts that are at all likely to be chafed should be well powdered. After the infant is well dried, the chest, the back, the bowels, and the limbs, should be gently rubbed, taking care not to expose the child unnecessarily during such friction. The infant should be partially washed every evening; indeed, it may be necessary to use a sponge and a little warm water frequently during the day. Cleanliness is one of the grandest incentives to health, and therefore cannot be too strongly insisted upon. If more attention were paid to this subject, infants would be more exempt from chaffings, eruptions, and consequent suffering, than they at present are. After the second month, if the infant be delicate, the addition of a teacupful of vinegar, or two handfuls of table salt, to the water he is washed with of a morning, will tend to brace and strengthen him. With regard to the best powder to dust infants with, there is nothing better for general use than starch reduced to a very fine powder, either by means of a pestle and mortar, or a smooth glass bottle. For occasional use, finely powdered Fuller's earth may with advantage be substituted. Hair powder is very often used for the purpose; but as it frequently contains lime it is improper, as lime is very irritating to the tender skin of an infant. Tutty is another preparation that should never be applied. Some mothers are in the habit of using white lead; but as it is a poison it should on no account be resorted to.

MANAGEMENT OF THE NAVEL.

4.—*Q.* Should the navel string be wrapped in singed rag?

A. There is nothing better than a piece of fine old linen rag, *unsinged:* when singed, it frequently irritates the infant's skin.

5.—*Q.* When does the navel string separate from the child?

A. From three days to a week after birth; in some cases, not until ten days or a fortnight.

6.—*Q.* If the navel string does not come away at the end of four or five days, should any means be used to cause its separation?

A. Certainly not. It should always be allowed to drop off, which, when in a fit state, it will readily do, by turning the infant over on his bowels. Meddling with the navel string has frequently cost the infant a great deal of suffering, and, in some cases, even his life.

7.—*Q.* Sometimes the navel is a little sore after the navel string comes away: what should then be done?

A. A little simple cerate should be spread on lint, and applied to the parts affected, every morning, and a little white-bread poultice every night, till it be quite healed.

CLOTHING.

8.—*Q.* Is it necessary to have a flannel cap in readiness, to put on as soon as an infant is born?

A. It is the safest plan; it frequently prevents inflammation of the eyes—a complaint to which new-born infants are very subject.

9.—*Q.* What kind of belly-band do you recommend, a flannel or calico one?

A. I prefer flannel, for two reasons: first, on account of its keeping the child's bowels comfortably warm; and secondly, on account of its not chilling the child (and thus endangering cold, &c.) when he wets himself.

10.—*Q.* Have you any remarks to make on the clothing of an infant?

A. An infant's clothing should be warm, loose, and free from pins. 1. *It should be warm* without being cumbersome. The parts that should be kept warm are, the chest, the bowels, and the feet. If the infant be delicate, especially if he should be subject to inflammation of the lungs, he should wear a fine flannel shirt instead of the usual ones, and which should be changed as frequently. 2. *The dress should be loose*, so as to prevent any pressure upon the blood-vessels, which would otherwise impede the circulation, and prevent a proper development of the parts. 3. As *few pins* should be used in dressing an infant as possible: inattention to this advice has caused many a little sufferer to be thrown into convulsions.

11.—*Q.* Is there much necessity for a nurse being very particular in airing an infant's clothes before they are put on? If she were not so very particular, would it not make an infant more hardy?

A. A nurse cannot be too particular on this head. Infants' clothes should be well aired the day before they are put on, as they should not be put on warm from the fire. It is well, where it can be done, to let infants have clean clothes every day; where this cannot be afforded, the clothes should be well aired as soon as they are taken off at night, so as to free them from perspiration, and to be in readiness to put on the following morning. It is truly nonsensical to endeavour to harden infants, or any one else, by putting on damp clothes.

12.—*Q.* What is your opinion of caps for infants?

A. The head should be kept cool, except when they are just born, and every time when they are washed. If caps be worn at all, they should only be so for the first month in summer, or the first two or three months in winter. If an infant takes to caps, it requires care in leaving them off, or he will take cold: when you are about discontinuing them, put a thinner and thinner one on every time they are changed, till you leave them off altogether.

DIET.

13.—*Q.* Are you an advocate for putting an infant to the breast soon after birth, or waiting, as many do, till the third day?

A. The infant should be put to the breast very soon after birth. The interest of the mother and child demand it. It will be advisable to wait three or four hours, that the mother may recover from her fatigue; and then the infant should be put to the breast. If such be done, the child will generally take the nipple with the greatest avidity. It may be said, at such an early period there is no milk in the breast; but such is not the case. There generally is *a little* from the very beginning, which acts on the infant's bowels like a dose of purgative medicine, and appears to be intended by nature to cleanse the system. But, provided there be no milk at first, the very act of sucking not only gives the child a notion, but, at the same time causes a draught (as it is usually called) in the breast, and enables the milk to flow easily. Those infants who are kept from the breast two or three days, and are fed upon gruel, generally become feeble, and frequently, at the end of that time, will not take the breast at all. Moreover, there is a thick cream (similar to the boistings of a cow), which, if not drawn out by the infant, causes inflammation and gathering of the breast, and, consequently, great suffering to the mother. A new-born infant should not have gruel given to him, as it disorders the bowels, causes a disinclination to suck, and thus makes him feeble.

14.—*Q.* Provided there be no milk *at first*, what should then be done?

A. Wait with patience. In the generality of instances, artificial food is not at all necessary. The infant should be put to the nipple every two hours, till he is able to find nourishment. We frequently hear of infants having no notion of sucking. This "no notion" may generally be traced to bad management, to stuffing children with food, and thus giving them a disinclination to take the nipple at all.

15.—*Q.* How often should a mother suckle her infant?

A. Mothers generally suckle their infants too often, having them almost constantly at the breast. This practice is injurious both to mother and child. For the first month the child should be suckled about every hour and a half; for the second month every two hours, gradually lengthening the distance of time between as the child becomes older, till at length he has it about every four hours. If infants were suckled at stated periods they would only look for the breast at those times, and be satisfied.

16.—*Q.* Where the mother is *moderately* strong, do you advise that the infant should have any other food than the breast?

A. Artificial food should not be given if the mother be *moderately* strong; of course, if the mother be very feeble, a little food will be necessary. Many delicate women enjoy better health whilst suckling than at any other time.

17.—*Q.* What food is the best substitute for a mother's milk?

A. The food that suits one infant will not agree with another. The one I have found the most generally useful is made as follows:—Boil the crumb of bread for four or five hours in water, taking particular care that it does not burn; then add only a *little* lump sugar, to make it palatable. When the infant is two or three months old add a little new milk, gradually increasing the quantity as the child becomes older, till it is nearly all milk, there being only enough water to boil the bread: the milk should not be boiled. If the above should not agree with the infant (although it almost invariably does, if properly made), take about a pound of flour, put it in a cloth, tie it up tightly, then put it in a saucepanful of water, and let it boil four or five hours; then take it out, peel off the outer rind, and the inside will be found quite dry, which grate. A small quantity of this boiled flour should be made into food in the same way as gruel is made, and then slightly sweetened with lump sugar. When the infant is two or three months old new milk, provided it agree with the child, may be added in a similar way to that recommended for boiled bread. A third food may be made with " Farinaceous Food for Infants, prepared by Hards, of Dartford." Whatever artificial food is used should be given with a bottle, not only as it is a more natural way of feeding an infant than any other, but as the act of sucking causes the salivary glands to press out their contents, which materially assists digestion. Moreover, it seems to satisfy the child more than it otherwise would. The food should be of the consistence of good cream, and should be made fresh and fresh. Great attention should be paid to the cleanliness of the vessel, and great care should be taken that the milk be new and of good quality; for if it be not so it will turn acid and sour, and curdle in the stomach, and will thus cause flatulence and looseness of the bowels, and perhaps convulsions. Very little sugar should be added to the food, as much sugar weakens the digestion.

18.—*Q.* Where it is found absolutely necessary to give an infant artificial food *whilst suckling*, how often should he be fed?

A. Not oftener than three times during the twenty-four hours, and then only in small quantities at a time, as the stomach requires rest, and at the same time can manage to digest a little food better than it can a great deal.

19.—*Q.* When the mother is not able to suckle her infant herself, what should be done?

A. It should first of all be ascertained beyond all doubt that a mother is not able to suckle her own child. Many delicate females do suckle their infants with advantage, not only to their offspring, but to themselves. Many mothers are never so well as when they are suckling; besides, suckling prevents women from becoming pregnant so frequently as they otherwise would. This is an important consideration if a female be delicate, and more especially if she be subject to miscarry. The effects of miscarriages are far more weakening than those of suckling. Not only so, but mothers should be actuated by nobler motives.* Hirelings, let them be ever so

* On this head, Montgomery speaks very justly in his beautiful poem, *On the Neglect of Maternal Duties in High Life.*

> " A mother's love!—resistless speaks that claim,
> When first the cherub lisps her gentle name!
> And looking up, it moves its little tongue,
> In passive dalliance to her bosom clung;
> 'Tis sweet to view the sinless baby rest,
> To drink its life-spring from her nursing breast;
> And mark the smiling mother's mantling eyes,
> While hush'd beneath, the helpless infant lies:
> How fondly pure that unobtruding pray'r,
> Breath'd gently o'er the listless sleeper there!
> 'Tis Nature this!—the forest beast can hug,
> And cubs are nestled 'neath its milky dug;
> But FASHION petrifies the HUMAN heart,
> Scar'd at her nod, see ev'ry love depart!
>
> In Rome's majestic days, long fleeted by,
> Did not her mighty dames sing lullaby?
> No mean-bred hags then nurs'd the guiltless child,
> No kitchen slang its innocence despoil'd;

well inclined, can never have the affection and unceasing assiduity of a parent, and therefore cannot perform the duties of lactation with equal advantage to the infant. If it be ascertained past all doubt that a mother cannot suckle her own child, then, if the circumstances of the parents will allow (and they should strain a point to accomplish it), a healthy wet nurse should be procured, as, of course, the food which Nature has supplied is far superior to any invented by art. But if a wet nurse cannot fill the place of a mother, then the food recommended in answer to No. 17 question may be given, with this only difference—a little new milk may be added from the beginning, and gradually increased till nearly all milk be used. Food should be given, for the first month, about every two hours; the second month, about every three hours, lengthening the space of time as the infant advances in age.

20.—*Q.* How would you choose a wet nurse?

A. I would inquire particularly into the state of her health; ascertain whether she be of a healthy family, whether she is of a consumptive habit, whether

> 'Twas deem'd a glory that the babe should rest
> In slumbering beauty on the MOTHER's breast;
> But ENGLAND's mighty dame is TOO GENTEEL
> To nurse, and guard, and like a mother feel!"

she or her family have laboured under king's evil, ascertaining if there be any seams or swellings about the neck; whether she has any eruptions or blotches upon the skin; whether she has a plentiful breast of milk, and if it be of good quality (which may be ascertained by milking a little into a glass); whether she has good nipples, sufficiently long for the child to hold; that they be not sore; and whether the child is of the same age, or nearly so, as the one you wish her to nurse. Indeed, if it be possible to procure such a one, she should be from the country, of ruddy complexion, clear skin, and between twenty and five-and-twenty years of age, as the milk will then be fresh, pure, and nourishing. I consider it of the greatest importance that the child of the wet nurse should be as nearly as possible of the same age as your own, as the milk varies in nourishment according to the age of the child. For instance, during the early period of suckling the milk is very thick and creamy, similar to the boistings of a cow, which, if given to a child of a few months old, would cause great derangement of the stomach and bowels.

21.—*Q*. What should be the diet of a wet nurse or of a mother who is suckling?

A. It is an usual practice to cram a wet nurse with food, and to give her strong ale to drink, to make good nourishment and plentiful milk! This practice is most absurd; for it either, by making the nurse feverish, makes the milk more sparing than usual, or it makes the milk gross and unwholesome. On the other hand, we should not run into an opposite extreme. The mother or wet nurse, by using those means most conducive to her own health, will best advance the interest of the infant. A wet nurse should live somewhat in the following way:—Let her have tea for her breakfast, with one or two slices of cold meat if her appetite demand it, but not otherwise. It is usual for wet nurses to make hearty luncheons: of this I do not approve. If they feel faint or low at eleven o'clock, let them have a tumbler of porter or mild fresh ale, with a piece of dry toast soaked in it. A nurse should not dine later than half-past one or two o'clock; she should eat for her dinner fresh mutton or beef, with a nice mealy potatoe and stale bread. Puddings, soups, gravies, high-seasoned dishes, salted meats, and green vegetables (unless it be, occasionally, a few asparagus heads, or brocoli, or cauliflower), should be carefully avoided, as they only tend to disorder the stomach, and deteriorate the milk. It is a common remark that "mothers who are suckling may eat any thing." I do not agree to this opinion. Can impure or improper food make pure and proper milk, or can impure or improper milk make good blood for an infant, and thus good health? The wet nurse may take a moderate quantity of good porter, or mild (but not old or strong) ale, with her dinner. Tea should be taken at half-past five or six, supper at nine; which should consist of a slice or two of cold meat, or cheese if she should prefer it, with half a pint of porter or mild ale: occasionally a basin of gruel may be taken with greater advantage. Hot and late suppers are most prejudicial to the mother or wet nurse, and, consequently, to the child. The wet nurse should be in bed every night by ten o'clock. It may be said I have been too minute and particular in my rules for a wet nurse; but when it is considered of what vital importance good milk is to the well-doing of an infant, in making him strong and robust, not only now, but as he grows up to manhood, I shall, I trust, be excused for my prolixity.

22.—*Q.* Have you any more hints to offer with regard to the management of a wet nurse?

A. A wet nurse is frequently allowed to remain in bed until a late hour in the morning, and to continue in the house during the day as if she were a fixture! How is it possible that any one, under such a practice, can continue healthy? A wet nurse should rise early and take a walk, if the weather and season will permit; which will give her a good appetite for her breakfast, and make a good meal for her little charge. Of course, this cannot be done during the winter months; but even then she should take every opportunity of walking out some part of the day; indeed, in the summer time, a nurse should live half her time in the open air. She should strictly avoid crowded rooms: her mind, also, should be kept calm and unruffled; for nothing disorders the milk so much as passion, or any other violent emotion of the mind; on which account you should endeavour, in choosing your wet nurse, to procure one of a mild, calm, and placid temper.

23.—*Q.* Have the goodness to state at what age a child should be weaned.

A. This, of course, must depend upon the strength of the child, and upon the health of the mother: on an average, nine months is the most proper time. If the mother be weak, it may be found necessary to wean the infant at six months; or if the child be weak, or be labouring under any disease, it may be well to continue suckling him for twelve months, but after that time the breast would do the child more harm than good, as well as, at the same time, injure the mother's health.

24.—*Q.* How would you recommend a mother to act when she weans her child?

A. She should do it gradually, as the word signifies—that is to say, she should by degrees give less and less of the breast, and more and more of artificial food; at length she should only suckle him at night; and, lastly, it would be well for the mother either to send the child away, or leave the child at home, and go away herself. A good plan is, for the nurse maid to have a half-pint bottle of new milk in the bed, so as to give a little to the child in lieu of the breast. The warmth of the body will keep the milk of a proper temperature, and will supersede the use of lamps, candle frames, and other contrivances.

25.—*Q.* Whilst a mother is weaning her infant, and after she has weaned him, what should be his diet?

A. Any of the food recommended in answer to Question 17, page 29.

26.—*Q.* If a child be suffering severely from wind, is there any objection to the addition of a very small quantity of gin or peppermint, to disperse it?

A. It is a murderous practice to add gin or peppermint of the shops (which is oil of peppermint dissolved in liquors) to the food. Many children have been made puny and delicate, and have gradually dropped into an untimely grave, by such practice. Those infants who are kept entirely to the breast— more especially if the mother be careful in her diet —seldom suffer from wind; those, on the contrary, who have much or improper artificial food,* suffer severely. Care in feeding, then, is the grand preventive against wind; but if, notwithstanding all your precautions, the child is troubled with flatulence, the remedies recommended in answer to Question 61, will generally answer the purpose.

27.—*Q.* Have you any remarks to make on sugar for sweetening infant's food?

A. The less sugar that is used in infant's food the better. Much sugar cloys the stomach, weakens the digestion, produces acidity, sour belchings, and wind.

---

* Never give artificial food to an infant who is suckling, if you can possibly avoid it. There is nothing agrees, in the generality of cases, like the mother's milk alone.

VACCINATION.

28.—Q. Are you an advocate for vaccination?

A. Most certainly. I consider it one of the greatest blessings ever conferred upon mankind. Before vaccination was adopted, smallpox ravaged the country like a plague, and carried off thousands annually; and those who did escape with their lives were frequently made loathsome and disgusting objects by it. Even inoculation (which is cutting for the smallpox) was attended with great danger.

29.—Q. But vaccination does not always protect a child from smallpox?

A. I grant you it does not *always* protect him from taking smallpox—*neither does inoculation;* but when a child is vaccinated, if he does take the smallpox, he is seldom pitted, and very rarely dies; and the disease assumes a comparatively mild form. There are a very few fatal cases recorded after vaccination, perhaps one in several thousands; but these may be considered only as exceptions to the general rule; and possibly some of these may be traced to the arm not having taken proper effect when the child was vaccinated. If children or adults were re-vaccinated, say in seven years after the first vaccination, depend upon it even these very rare cases would not occur.

30.—*Q.* Then do you consider it the duty of a parent, in all cases, to have their children vaccinated a second time after they have attained the age of seven years?

A. I do, most decidedly; as then they would be out of all danger from smallpox.

31.—*Q.* Are you not likely to take, not only the cowpox, but any other disease that the child has from whom the matter is taken?

A. The same objection holds good in cutting for smallpox, only in a tenfold degree, smallpox being such a disgusting complaint. Of course your medical attendant will be careful to take the matter from a healthy child.

32.—*Q.* At what age do you recommend an infant to be first vaccinated?

A. As soon after six weeks as possible, as the sooner an infant is protected the better. Moreover, the older a child is the greater difficulty there will be to prevent the arm from being rubbed, and thereby breaking the vesicles, and interfering with its effects.

If the smallpox is very prevalent, the infant may be vaccinated at the month's end with perfect safety.

33.—*Q.* If the infant has any breaking out upon the skin, should that be a reason for deferring the vaccination?

A. It should, as two skin diseases cannot well go on together; hence the cowpox might not take, or, if it take, might not have its proper effect in preventing smallpox. But the moment the skin is free from the breaking out, the infant should be vaccinated.

34.—*Q.* Do you approve of giving the infant medicine after vaccination?

A. No: as it would be likely to work off some of its effects. I do not like to interfere with it, but to allow it to have full power upon the constitution.

DENTITION.

35.—*Q.* At what time does dentition commence?
A. The period at which it commences is very uncertain. As a general rule, it may be said, an infant begins to cut his teeth at seven months old.

Some have cut teeth at three months; indeed, there are instances on record of infants having been born with teeth. King Richard III. is said to have been an example. Shakspere notices it thus:—

"YORK.—Marry, they say, my uncle grew so fast,
That he could gnaw a crust at two hours old;
'Twas full two years ere I could get a tooth.
Grandam, this would have been a biting jest."

Act II., Scene 5th.

Where children are born with teeth, those teeth generally drop out. On the other hand, teething, in some children, does not commence until they are eighteen months or two years old.

36.—*Q.* What is the number of the first set of teeth, and in what order do they generally appear?

A. The first set consists of twenty. The two lower front teeth usually make their appearance first, then the two upper ones, then the remainder of the lower front, then the remainder of the upper front, then the first grinders in the lower jaw, then the first upper grinders, then the lower corner teeth, then the upper corner or eye-teeth, then the second grinders in the lower jaw, and, lastly, the second grinders of the upper jaw. Of course, they do not always appear in this order: nothing is more uncertain than teething. A child seldom cuts his second grinders till he is two years old.

37.—*Q.* If a child be feverish, irritable, or otherwise poorly, and the gums be swollen, are you an advocate for their being lanced?

A. Most certainly, as by doing so the child will, in the generality of instances, be almost instantly relieved.

38.—*Q.* But it has been stated that lancing of the gums hardens them.

A. It has a contrary effect. It is a well-known fact that a part which has been divided gives way much more readily than one that has not been so. Again, the tooth is bound down by a tight membrane, which, if not released by lancing, frequently brings on convulsions.

39.—*Q.* If teething causes convulsions, what should be done?

A. The first thing to be done is, to put the child into a warm bath* of 98° Fah. If a thermometer

---

* For the precautions to be used in putting a child into a warm bath, see the answer to Question 145.

be not at hand,* the mother should put her elbow in the water; a comfortable heat for the elbow will be a proper heat for the child. The child should remain in the bath for a quarter of an hour, or till the fit is at an end. The gums should then be lanced, and cold vinegar and water should be applied to the head. As soon as the child comes to himself a dose of aperient medicine should be given.

40.—*Q.* Nurses are in the habit of giving children coral or ivory, during teething, to bite: do you approve of the practice?

A. I think it a bad practice to give the child any hard, unyielding substance, as it tends to harden the gums, and by so doing causes the teeth to come through with greater difficulty. I have found softer substances of great service—such as a piece of wax taper, a piece of India rubber, a piece of the best bridle leather, a portion of liquorice root, or a crust of bread.

41.—*Q.* Do you approve of giving a child much fruit during teething?

---

* No family, where there are young children, should be without Fahrenheit's thermometer.

A. No: unless it be a few ripe strawberries, or a roasted apple, or the juice of two or three grapes—taking care he does not swallow the seeds or the skin—or the inside of a nice ripe gooseberry. Such fruits will be particularly indicated, if the bowels are in a costive state. All stone fruits, raw apples or pears, should be carefully avoided, as they not only disorder the stomach and bowels (causing convulsions, gripings, &c.), but they have the effect of weakening the bowels, and thus of producing worms.

42.—*Q.* Are children more subject to disease during teething? and, if so, to what diseases? and in what manner may they be prevented?

A. Dentition is one of the most important periods of a child's life, and brings more diseases in its train than anything else; therefore, during teething, a child requires constant watching. The complaints or diseases induced by dentition are almost without number, affecting almost every organ of the body—the *brain*, causing convulsions, water on the brain, &c.; the *lungs*, producing inflammation, cough, &c.; the *stomach*, causing sickness, flatulence, acidity, &c.; the *bowels*, inducing griping, at one time costiveness, and at another time looseness. To prevent these diseases, means should be used to invigorate a child's constitution by plain wholesome food, as recommended under the article of diet; by exercise and fresh air, by lancing the gums when they are very red and much swollen, by attention to the bowels (if the child suffer more than usual, by keeping them rather in a relaxed state by any simple aperient, such as castor oil, magnesia and rhubarb, &c.), and, let me add, by attention to the temper; many children are made feverish and ill by petting and spoiling them. On this subject, I cannot do better than refer you to an excellent little work entitled Abbot's *Mother at Home*, wherein he proves the great importance of early training.

Q. Should a child be purged violently during teething, or, indeed, during any other time, do you approve of absorbent medicines to restrain it?

A. Certainly not; I should look upon the relaxation as an effort of Nature to relieve itself. A child is never purged without a cause; that cause, in the generality of instances, is the presence of some undigested food, acidity, or depraved motions that want a vent. In such cases, the better plan is to give a dose of aperient medicine, such as castor oil, or magnesia and rhubarb, and thus work it off. If we lock up the bowels we lock up the enemy, and thus produce great mischief.

44.—*Q.* Children are very subject to slight coughs during dentition, called by nurses "tooth-cough," which a parent would not consider of sufficient importance to consult a medical man about: pray tell me, is there any objection to a mother giving her child a small quantity of syrup of poppies to ease it?

A. A cough is an effort of Nature to bring up any little secretion from the lining membrane of the lungs, and hence it should not be interfered with. I have known the administration of syrup of poppies stop the cough, and thereby prevent the expulsion of the phlegm, and thus produce inflammation of the lungs.

45.—*Q.* Children who are teething are very subject to an eruption, more especially behind the ears, which is very disfiguring and frequently very annoying: what would you recommend?

A. I would apply no external application to cure it, as I should look upon it as an effort of the constitution to relieve itself, and should expect, if it were repelled, that convulsions, or inflammation of the lungs, or water on the brain, would be the consequence. The only plan I would adopt would be to be more careful in the child's diet; to give him less meat, and to give a few doses of mild aperient medicine once or twice a week; and if the irritation from the eruption be very great, to bathe it occasionally with a little warm milk and water, or rose-water.

EXERCISE.

46.—*Q.* Do you recommend exercise in the open air for an infant? and, if so, how soon after birth?

A. I am a great advocate for exercise in the open air for infants. The length of time after birth it should be carried into execution will, of course, depend upon the season, and upon the weather. If it be summer, and the weather be fine, the infant may be taken in the open air a fortnight after birth; but if it be winter, he should not on any account be taken out under the month, and not even then, unless the day be mild for the season, and during the middle of the day. At the end of two months the infant may be taken out more frequently. At the end of three months he should be carried out every day, even if it should be wet under foot, provided it be fine above, and the wind be not in an easterly direction; by doing so we shall make the infant strong and hearty, and give the skin that mottled appearance which is so characteristic of health. Of course, the child should be well clothed.

47.—Q. Do you approve of tossing an infant much about?

A. Violent tossing of a young infant should never be allowed; it only frightens him, and has been known to bring on fits. He should be gently moved up and down (not tossed): such exercise causes a proper circulation of the blood, promotes digestion, and soothes to sleep. He should be always kept quiet after taking the breast; if he be tossed directly afterwards it interferes with digestion, and is likely to produce sickness.

SLEEP.

48.—Q. Should the infant's sleeping apartments be kept warm?

A. The lying-in room is generally kept too warm, its heat being, in many instances, more that of an oven than of a room. Such a place is most unhealthy, and fraught with great danger both to mother and infant. Of course, we are not to run into an opposite extreme, but we are to keep the room of a moderate and comfortable temperature. An infant should not be allowed to look at the glare of the fire or at a lighted candle, as they tend to weaken the sight, and sometimes bring on inflammation of the eyes.

49.—*Q.* Should an infant lie alone from the first.

A. Certainly not. At first (say for the first nine months) he requires the warmth of another person's body, especially in the winter; but afterwards he had better lie alone on a horse-hair or oat-chaff* mattress.

50.—*Q.* Do you approve of rocking an infant to sleep?

A. I do not. If the rules of health be attended to, the infant will sleep soundly and sweetly without rocking; if they be not attended to, the rocking might cause the child to fall into a feverish, disturbed slumber, but not into a refreshing, calm sleep. Besides, if you once take to that habit, the child will not go to sleep without it.

51.—*Q.* Do you advise the head of a crib to be covered with a handkerchief while the infant is

---

* For directions respecting the preparing of oat chaff for mattresses, see the answer to the 119th question.

asleep, to shade the eyes from the light, and, if it be summer-time, to keep off the flies?

A. If the head of the crib be covered, the infant cannot breathe freely; the air within becomes contaminated, and thus the lungs cannot properly perform their functions. If his sleep is to be refreshing he must breathe pure, fresh air. I do not even approve of a head to a crib. Many infants are allowed to sleep on a bed with the curtains drawn completely close, as though it were dangerous for a breath of air to blow upon them! This practice is most injurious. An infant should have the full benefit of the air of the room; indeed, the bed-room door should be frequently left ajar, so that the air of the apartment might be changed, of course taking care not to expose him to a draught.

52.—*Q.* Is it a good sign for a young infant to sleep much?

A. Infants who sleep a great deal thrive much more than those who do not; indeed, sleep appears to do them more good than any thing else. I have known many new-born infants who were born small and delicate, but who slept the greatest part of their time, become strong, healthy children. On the other hand, I have known infants who were born large and strong, but who slept but little, become weak and unhealthy. The practice of nurses allowing children to sleep upon their laps is a bad one, and should never be countenanced. A child sleeps cooler, more comfortably and soundly, in his crib.

53.—*Q.* How is it that much sleep causes young infants to thrive so well?

A. If there be pain in any part of the body, or if any of the functions be not properly performed, the infant sleeps but little. On the contrary, if there be exemption from pain, and if there be a due performance of all the functions, he sleeps a great deal; and thus the body becomes refreshed and invigorated.

54.—*Q.* As much sleep is of such great advantage, if a young infant sleeps but little, would you advise composing medicine to be given to him?

A. Certainly not. The practice of giving composing medicines to young children cannot be too strongly reprobated. If a child does not sleep sufficiently, the mother should ascertain if the bowels are in a proper state, that they are sufficiently open, and that the motions are of a good colour (namely, a bright yellow), and free from slime. An occasional dose of rhubarb and magnesia is frequently the best composing medicine for an infant.

AILMENTS, &c.

55.—*Q.* New-born infants frequently have a collection of mucus in the air-passages, causing them to wheeze: is it a dangerous symptom?

A. No; not if it occurs immediately after birth: it generally leaves them as soon as the bowels have been opened. If there be any mucus about the mouth, impeding breathing, it should be removed with a soft handkerchief.

56.—*Q.* Is it advisable to give an infant medicine as soon as he is born? and, if so, what medicine is the best?

A. It is doubtful whether medicine be at all necessary immediately after birth, provided the infant be early put to the breast, as the mother's first milk is generally sufficient to open the bowels. A common practice among nurses is to give rue tea, or butter and sugar. There is no objection to either of them, but, if medicine be given at all, half a teaspoonful of castor oil will perhaps be the best.

57.—*Q.* Have the goodness to mention the slight ailments which are not of sufficient importance to demand the assistance of a medical man.

A. I think it well to make the distinction between serious and slight ailments: I am now addressing mothers. With regard to serious ailments, I do not think myself justified in instructing a parent to deal with them. I consider much mischief has been inflicted by popular works on the treatment of *serious* diseases of children; and I do hereby enter my strongest protest against such works. Serious diseases should never be treated by a parent, not even in the early stages; for it is in the early stages that most good can generally be done. It is utterly impossible for a person not trained up to the medical profession to understand a serious disease in all its bearings, and thereby to treat it successfully. The trifling ailments of infants, and which may be treated by a parent, are the following:—Chafings, Costiveness, Flatulence, Hiccup, Looseness of the Bowels, Red Gum, " Snuffles," Sickness, Thrush.

58.—*Q.* What are the causes of Chafing, and what is its treatment?

A. Inattention and want of cleanliness are the frequent causes of chafing. The chafed parts should be sponged with tepid rain water, and afterwards well dried with a soft towel, and powdered.

59.—*Q.* What are the best remedies for Costiveness in infants?

A. I strongly object to the constant administration of opening medicines, as the frequent repetition of them increases the mischief to a tenfold degree. It might be necessary occasionally to give a little opening medicine, and when it is necessary the following will be found to have the desired effect:—Take half a drachm of powdered Turkey rhubarb, two scruples of pure carbonate of magnesia, two drachms of simple syrup, and ten drachms of aniseed water. Let them be well mixed together, and let one or two teaspoonfuls be given at bedtime occasionally. Another excellent remedy for the costiveness of infants is a soap suppository, the application of which will be found a safe, speedy, and certain method of opening the bowels. It may be made by paring a piece of white soap round, rather larger than a tobacco-pipe in circumference, and about an inch and a half or two inches in length. It may be administered by dipping it in a little warm water, and then gently introducing it up the bowels in the same manner you would a glyster pipe. In a minute or two the infant's bowels will be comfortably and effectually opened. It is a common practice in this country to give calomel, on account of the readiness by which it may be administered, it being small in quantity, and nearly tasteless. This practice cannot be too strongly reprobated, as the constant giving of mercury weakens the body, predisposes it to cold, and frequently excites king's evil—a disease too common in this country. Calomel should never be given, unless directed by a medical man. Senna tea and jalap are also given, but they are griping remedies. Castor oil is another medicine given in costiveness, and, it being a safe one, may be used occasionally, mixed with a little sugar or simple syrup. A roasted apple, mixed with a little sugar, is another simple and safe aperient. The frequent repetition of opening medicines very much interferes with digestion, and should, therefore, be given as seldom as possible.

60.—*Q.* Are there any means of preventing the costiveness of infants?

A. If greater attention were paid to the rules of health—such as attention to diet, exercise in the open air, and the regular habit of causing the infant to be held out at stated periods, whether he wants or not, that he may solicit a stool, costiveness would not so frequently prevail.

61.—*Q.* What are the causes of, and remedies for, Flatulence?

A. Flatulence more frequently occurs in those infants who live on artificial food, especially if they be overfed. I therefore beg to refer you to the precautions I have given when speaking of the times of feeding, and of the best kinds of artificial food, and of those which are least likely to cause wind. Notwithstanding these precautions, if the infant should still suffer from flatulence, a little aniseed may be added to the food:—Take three drops of oil of aniseed, or oil of dill, and two lumps of sugar; rub them well in a mortar together. Then add, drop by drop, three tablespoonfuls of spring water—a teaspoonful of this may be added to each quantity of food; or two or three teaspoonfuls of carraway seeds may be boiled in a teacupful of water for ten minutes, and then strained—one or two teaspoonfuls of the carraway tea may be added to each quantity of food; or a dose of rhubarb and magnesia may be occasionally given. Godfrey's Cordial and Dalby's Carminative are frequently given in flatulence; but as most of these quack medicines contain opium in one form or another, and as opium is a most dangerous remedy for infants, all quack medicines should be banished the nursery. Although I strongly object to the *internal* administration of opium, yet its *external* application frequently gives an infant labouring under pains of the stomach and bowels, from flatulence, instant relief. The laudanum liniment (linimentum opii) is the best of the kind, and should be well rubbed over the stomach and bowels till relief be obtained. A warm bath (where the infant is suffering severely) frequently affords great ease in flatulence: it acts as a fomentation to the bowels. But, after all, a dose of mild aperient medicine is oftentimes the best treatment for " wind." Remember, at all times, prevention, where it is possible, is better than cure.

62.—*Q.* What is the cause of Hiccup, and what is its treatment?

A. Hiccup is of such a trifling nature as hardly to require interference. It may be generally traced to overfeeding. Should it be very severe, four or five grains of calcined magnesia, with a little syrup and aniseed water, will be all that is necessary.

63.—*Q.* What is the cause of "Looseness of the Bowels," and what is its treatment?

A. The cause is some acidity or vitiated stool that wants a vent, and thus endeavours to obtain one by purging. The best treatment is to assist Nature by giving a dose of castor oil, and thus working it off.

64.—*Q.* What are the symptoms of Red Gum, and what is its treatment?

A. It consists of several small papulæ or pimples, about the size of pin's heads, and may be known from measles (the only disease with which it is at all likely to be mistaken) by its being unattended with symptoms of cold, such as sneezing, running and redness of the eyes, &c.; in short, red gum may be readily known by the child's health being perfectly unaffected. Little need be done: if there be a good deal of irritation, a mild aperient may be given. The child should be kept moderately warm, but not hot. Draughts of air or cold should be carefully avoided, as, by sending the eruption suddenly in, convulsions or disordered bowels may be produced.

65.—*Q.* How would you prevent " Snuffles" in a new-born infant?

A. He should have a flannel cap put on his head the moment he is born. This should be worn every time he is washed. Rubbing a little tallow on the bridge of the nose is the old-fashioned remedy, and answers every purpose. If the " snuffles" be very bad, dip a sponge in hot water (as hot as the child can comfortably bear), and apply it for a few minutes to the bridge of the nose. As soon as the filth which produces the "snuffles" is within reach, it should be carefully removed.

66.—*Q.* Do you consider sickness injurious to an infant?

A. Many thriving infants are frequently sick after taking the breast; but yet we cannot look upon sickness otherwise than an index of either a disordered or an overloaded stomach. If the child be sick and yet thrives, it is a proof that he overloads his stomach. A mother should then not allow him to suck so much at a time. She should lessen the quantity of milk till the child retains all he takes. If the child be sick, and does *not* thrive, the mother should then ascertain if the milk he throws up is sour and curdled. If it be, the mother must first of all look to her own health; she must ascertain if her own stomach be out of order, for if it be it is impossible for her to make good milk. She should notice whether her tongue is furred and dry of a morning; whether she has a disagreeable taste in her mouth; if she has pains at her stomach, heartburn, or flatulence. If she has all or either of these symptoms, the mystery is explained why the child is sick and does not thrive. She should then seek advice, and her medical attendant will soon put her stomach into good order, and by so doing will put the child's likewise. But if the mother be in the enjoyment of good health we must then look to the child; ascertain if he be cutting his teeth, if the gums require lancing, if the secretions from the bowels are proper in quantity and in quality, and if the child has had *artificial* food (it being absolutely necessary to give such food), whether it agrees with the child. In the first place, let the gums be lanced; in the second place, give a dose of aperient medicine, such as castor oil, or the following:—Take two or three grains of powdered Turkey rhubarb, three grains of pure carbonate of magnesia, and one grain of aromatic powder: mix. The powder to be taken at bedtime, in a teaspoonful of sugar and water, and repeated the following night, if necessary. In the third place, change the artificial food (vide answer to Question 17), give it in smaller quantities at a time, and not so frequently, or, what would be better still, if it be possible, keep the child, for a few days at least, entirely to the breast.

67.—*Q.* What are the causes, symptoms, prevention, and cure of Thrush?

A. The thrush is a very frequent disease of infants, and is often brought on by stuffing them, or giving them improper food. It consists of several white vesicles on the lips, tongue, and inside of the mouth, giving the parts affected the appearance of curds and whey having been smeared upon them. Sometimes, although but rarely, the thrush runs through the whole of the alimentary canal. It should be borne in mind that nearly all children who are suckling have their tongues white, or frosted, as it is sometimes called. The thrush may be very mild or very severe. When *mild*, it will readily yield to the following treatment :—Mix equal parts of castor oil and of simple syrup together, say of each half an ounce; of this mixture give a teaspoonful twice or three times a day. The best local application to the parts will consist of an equal proportion of powdered lump sugar and borax, which should be well mixed together; a little of this powder to be smeared with the finger upon the parts frequently. Under the above treatment, if the disease be mild, it will readily disappear. If the thrush be brought on by too much or improper food, in the first case, of course, a mother should lessen the quantity; and in the second case she should be more careful in her selection. When the disease is severe it may require more active treatment, such as a dose or two of calomel; which medicine should never be given, unless under the direction of a medical man; therefore, in such cases, a mother had better seek advice.

68.—*Q.* If an infant be delicate, have you any objection to his having beef tea or mutton broth to strengthen him?

A. Beef tea, mutton, or any other broth, seldom agree with an infant at the breast. I have known them to produce sickness, disorder the bowels, and create fever. I should strongly recommend you, therefore, not to make the attempt. Although broths, &c., when taken by the mouth, will seldom agree with infants at the breast, yet, when used as glysters, and in small quantities, so that they may be retained, I have frequently found them to be of the greatest benefit; they have appeared, in some instances, to have snatched delicate children from the brink of the grave.

69.—*Q.* Sometimes there is great difficulty in restraining the bleeding of leech-bites: what is the best method of doing so?

A. The great difficulty in these cases generally proceeds from the improper method of performing it. For example, a mother endeavours to stop the hæmorrhage by loading the part with rag; the more it discharges the more rag she puts on. At the same time the child is in a room with a large fire, and two or three candles, and a closed door, and perhaps a dozen people in the room, whom the mother has sent for in her fright. This practice is strongly reprehensible. If the bleeding cannot be stopped, in the first place, the fire should be lessened, the door should be thrown open, the room should be cleared of persons, with the exception of one, or at farthest two; every rag should be removed, and fur from a hat should then be firmly pressed with the finger, for a quarter of an hour at least, over the bleeding orifice. If this should not have the desired effect, a piece of lint about the size of the little finger nail should be applied over the part; over which a pad of lint about a quarter of an inch thick, and about the size of a sixpence in circumference, should be strapped firmly on it with narrow strips of adhesive plaister, which should cross and recross each other in every direction: this plan, if properly executed, never fails. Many infants have lost their lives by excessive loss of blood from leech-bites, from a mother not knowing how to act, and from the medical man living at a distance, or not being at hand.

70.—*Q.* Suppose an infant be poorly, have you any advice to give to the mother as to her own management?

A. She should endeavour to calm her feelings, otherwise her milk will be disordered, and she will thus materially increase the infant's illness. If her child be labouring under any inflammatory disorder, she should refrain from beer, wine, and spirits, and from all stimulating food, otherwise she will feed his disease.

PART II.—CHILDHOOD.

ADVICE TO MOTHERS.

PART II.—CHILDHOOD.

ABLUTION.

71.—*Question.* At twelve months old, do you recommend a child to be put *in a tub* to be washed?

Answer. I do; so that the child's skin may be well and thoroughly cleansed. The head should be washed before the child is placed in his tub; then a large sponge should be well filled with the water and squeezed over the head, so that the water may stream over the whole surface of the body.

72.—*Q.* Some mothers object to a child standing in the water.

A. If the head be wetted before the child is placed in the tub, and the child be washed as above directed, I can myself see no valid objection to it.

The child should not be allowed to remain in the tub more than five minutes.

73.—*Q.* Does not washing the child's head every morning make him more liable to cold, and weaken the sight?

A. It does neither one nor the other; on the contrary, it prevents cold and strengthens the sight; it cleanses the scalp, prevents scurf, and by that means causes a more beautiful head of hair. The head should be well brushed with a soft brush after each washing, but not combed. The brushing causes a healthy circulation of the scalp.

74.—*Q.* Do you recommend a child to be washed *in his tub* night and morning?

A. No: once a day is quite sufficient; in the morning in preference to the evening.

75.—*Q.* Should a child be placed in his tub in a state of perspiration?

A. Of course he should not whilst perspiring violently, or it would be checked suddenly, and ill consequences would ensue; *nor should he be put in his tub when cold,* or his blood would be chilled, and sent from the skin to some internal vital part, and thus would be likely to light up inflammation, probably of the lungs. The child's skin, when he is placed in his bath, should be moderately and comfortably warm; neither too hot nor too cold.

76.—*Q.* When the child is a *year* old, do you recommend cold or warm water to be used?

A. If it be winter, a little warm water should be added, so as to raise the temperature to that of new milk. As the summer advances, less and less warm water is required; so that at length none is wanted.

77.—*Q.* If a child be delicate, do you recommend any thing to be added to the water, which may tend to brace and strengthen him?

A. Let two handfuls of table salt be dissolved in the water he is washed in of a morning; or, for a change, a breakfast-cupful of vinegar may be substituted for the salt.

78.—*Q.* Do you recommend the child to be rubbed with the hand after he has been dried with the towel?

A. I do; as friction encourages the cutaneous circulation, and causes the skin to perform its functions properly: thus preventing the perspiration (which is one of the impurities of the body) from being sent inwardly to the lungs, or other parts. The back, the chest, and the limbs, are the parts that should be well rubbed.

CLOTHING.

79.—*Q.* Have you any remarks to make on the clothing of a child?

A. The clothing of a child should be large and full in every part, and free from tight strings; so that the circulation of the blood may not be impeded, and that there may be plenty of room for the full developement of the rapidly growing body. The practice of some mothers, allowing their children to wear tight clothes, is truly reprehensible.

80.—What parts of the body in particular should be kept warm?

A. The chest, the bowels, and the feet, should be kept comfortably so. We must guard against an opposite extreme, and not keep them too hot. The head alone should be kept cool; on which account I do not approve of night-caps.

81.—*Q.* Do you approve of children wearing flannel night-gowns?

A. Children frequently throw the clothes off them, and have occasion to be taken up in the night, and, if they have not flannel shirts on, are likely to take cold; on which account I recommend them to be worn. Calico night-gowns should be worn over them.

82.—*Q.* Do you advise a child to be lightly clad, that he may be hardened thereby?

A. I should fear such a plan, instead of hardening, would be likely to produce contrary effects. It is a well-known fact that more children of the poor, who are thus lightly clad, die, than those who are properly defended from cold. What holds good with a young plant is equally applicable to a young child; and we all know it is ridiculous to think of unnecessarily exposing tender plants, to harden them. If they were thus exposed, they would wither and die!

83.—*Q.* If a child be delicate, or if he be predisposed to inflammation of the lungs, do you approve of his wearing flannel instead of linen shirts?

A. I do; as flannel tends to keep the body at an equal temperature—thus obviating the effects of the sudden changes of the weather—and promotes, by gentle friction, the cutaneous circulation. Of course, fine flannel should be used.

DIET.

84.—*Q*. At *twelve* months old, have you any objection to a child having any other food besides that you mentioned in answer to the 17th question?

A. There is no objection to his *occasionally* having for his dinner a mealy, mashed potatoe and gravy, or a few crumbs of bread and gravy. A little rice pudding, or batter pudding, may be given for a change; but remember, the food recommended before is what must be principally given till after a child is eighteen months old?

85.—*Q*. At *eighteen* months old, have you any objection to a child taking meat?

A. He should not take meat till he has several teeth to chew it with. If he has most of his teeth (which he most likely will have at this age) there is no objection to his taking a small slice of mutton, or occasionally of beef, which should be well cut in small pieces, and should be mixed with a nice mealy mashed potatoe, and a few crumbs of bread and gravy, either *every* day if he be delicate, or every *other* day, if he be a gross or fast-feeding child. It may be well, in the generality of cases, for the first few months, to give him meat *every other* day, and potatoe and gravy, or rice or batter pudding, on the alternate days.

86.—*Q.* Are you partial to puddings for children?

A. Fruit puddings and pastry are objectionable, but rice or batter puddings, or even Yorkshire pudding from under the meat, mixed with crumbs of bread, may be given in lieu of meat once or twice a-week.

87.—*Q.* As soon as a child has cut the whole of his first set of teeth, what should be his diet? What should be his breakfast?

A. He can then have nothing better, where milk agrees, than scalding hot new milk poured on sliced bread, with a slice or two of bread and butter to eat with it. Milk is a valuable diet for children; it is very nourishing, wholesome, and digestible. New milk, or new milk and water, should be used in preference either to cream or skim milk. The first is too rich for the delicate stomach of a child; the second is too poor, when robbed of the cream.

88.—*Q.* What should be his dinner?

A. He should now have meat every day, either fresh mutton or beef; which should be cut up very fine, and mixed with a mealy potatoe and gravy. He should be watched closely, to see that he well masticates his food, and that he does not eat too quickly.

89.—*Q.* Have you any objection to pork for a change?

A. I have the greatest objection to it. It is a rich, gross, and therefore unwholesome food for the delicate stomachs of children. I have known it, in several instances, produce violent pain, sickness, purging, and convulsions. It being a gross meat, if a child be fed much upon it, it will be likely to produce eruptions on the skin. In fine, the child's blood will put on the same character as the food it is fed with.

90.—*Q.* Have you any objection to veal for a child?

A. The objection to pork was that it was rich and gross: this does not hold good with veal; but the great objection to it is that it is very hard of digestion.

91.—*Q.* Do you disapprove of salt or boiled beef for a child?

A. They are also difficult of digestion, and should not be given.

92.—*Q.* Suppose, then, there is nothing on the table which a child may eat with impunity.

A. He should then have either a grilled mutton chop or a lightly-boiled egg; indeed, the latter, at any time, makes an excellent change.

93.—*Q.* Are potatoes an unwholesome food for children?

A. New potatoes are, but old potatoes, well cooked and mealy, are the best vegetables a child can have. They should be well mashed, as I have known lumps of potatoes cause convulsions.

94.—*Q.* Do you approve of any other vegetables for a child?

A. I do not, except it be occasionally a few asparagus heads.

95.—*Q.* But may not a mother be too particular in dieting a child?

A. Certainly not. If blood can be too pure and good, she may be so. When we take into account that the food we eat is converted into blood, that if the food be good the blood is good and that if the food be improper or impure the blood is impure likewise; and, moreover, when we know that every part of the body is formed by the blood, we cannot be considered too particular in making our selection of food. Besides, if undigestible or improper food be taken into the stomach, the blood will not only be made impure, but the stomach and bowels will be disordered.

96.—*Q.* What should a child drink with his dinner?

A. A little plain toast and water. Some parents are in the habit of giving their children beer with their dinners, making them live as they live themselves. This practice is truly absurd, and fraught with great danger; not only so, but it is inducing a child to be fond of that which in after life may be his bane and curse. No good end can be obtained by it; it will not strengthen so young a child: on the contrary, it will create fever and thereby weaken him, it will act injuriously upon his delicate nervous and vascular systems; and may thus be a means of producing inflammation of the brain or its membranes, and cause water on the brain—a disease to which young children are very subject—or induce inflammation of the lungs.

97.—*Q.* What should a child who has cut his teeth have for his supper?

A. The same as he has for his breakfast. He should sup at six o'clock.

98.—*Q.* If a child be delicate, is there any objection to a little wine, such as cowslip or tent, to strengthen him?

A. Wine should not be given to children; it is even more injurious than beer. Wine, beer, and liquors, principally owe their strength to the spirits of wine they contain.

99.—*Q.* Suppose a child suddenly loses his appetite, is any notice to be taken of it?

A. If a child cannot eat well, depend upon it there is something wrong about the system. If a child be teething, let a mother look well to the gums, and satisfy herself that they do not require lancing. If the gums are not inflamed, and no tooth appears near, let her look well to the state of the bowels; let her ascertain if they be sufficiently open, and that the stools be of a proper colour. If they be neither one or the other, give a dose of aperient medicine, which will generally put all to rights again. If the gums be right, and the bowels be right, and the child's appetite continues bad, call in assistance. A child asking for something to eat, is frequently the first favourable symptom in a severe illness; we may generally then prognosticate that all will soon be well again.

100.—*Q.* When a child is four or five years old, have you any objection to tea?

A. Some parents are in the habit of giving their children strong (and frequently green) tea. Now this practice is most hurtful. It acts injuriously upon their delicate nervous system, and thus weakens the whole frame. If milk does not agree, very weak tea—that is to say, water with a dash of black tea in it—may be substituted for the milk; but a mother should never give tea where milk or milk and water agree.

101.—*Q.* Should a boy of seven or eight years old take beer with his meals?

A. No: he should only take toast and water. Boys do not require such stimulants; indeed, at that tender age, they are decidedly injurious.

102.—Have you any objection to a child occasionally having cakes or sweetmeats?

A. I consider them as so much slow poison. Such things cloy and weaken the stomach, and thereby take away the appetite, and thus debilitate the frame. If a child is never allowed to eat such things, he will consider a piece of dry bread a luxury.

103.—*Q.* Is bakers' or home-made bread the most wholesome for children?

A. Bakers' bread is certainly the lightest, and, if we could depend upon its being unadulterated, would, from its lightness, be the most wholesome; but, as we cannot always depend upon bakers' bread, as a general rule, home-made bread should be preferred. If it be at all heavy, children should not be allowed to eat it; a baker's loaf should then be sent for, till light home-made bread can be procured. Heavy bread is most indigestible. Children should not be allowed to eat bread until it is two or three days old. If it be a week old, in cool weather, it will be the more wholesome.

104.—*Q.* Do you approve of carraway seeds or currants in bread or cakes; the former to disperse wind, the latter to open the bowels?

A. There is nothing better than plain bread: the carraway seeds generally pass through the bowels undigested; and thus may irritate and produce, instead of disperse wind. Some mothers put currants in cakes, with a view of opening the bowels; but they only open them by disordering them.

105.—*Q.* Is there any objection to butter for children?

A. I myself can see no objection to it; on the contrary, if the child be healthy, I consider bread and butter more nourishing than dry bread, provided the butter be used with moderation. Of course, if too much be given, it will disorder the child's stomach and produce sickness.

NURSERY.

106.—*Q.* Have you any remarks to make on the ventilation of a nursery?

A. The windows should be thrown up whenever the child is not in the nursery; indeed, when he is in, if the weather be fine, the upper sash may be lowered a little. A child should be made to change the room frequently, so that it may be freely ventilated; for good air is as necessary to a child's health as good food, and air cannot be good if it be not frequently changed.

107.—*Q.* Have you any observations to make on the *light* of a nursery?

A. A room cannot be too light. The windows of a nursery are generally too small. A child requires as much light as a plant. Gardeners are well aware of the great importance of light in the construction of their greenhouses; and yet children, who require it as much, and are of much greater importance, are cooped up in dark rooms.

108.—*Q.* Have you any more hints to offer conducive to the well-doing of my child?

A. You cannot be too particular in the choice of those who are in constant attendance upon him. You should be particularly careful in the selection of his nurse. She should be steady, lively, and good-tempered, and should be free from any natural defect, such as squinting, stammering, &c.; for children are such imitative creatures that they are likely to acquire that which in the nurse may be natural. She should be strong and active, so that the child might have plenty of good nursing. She should never be allowed to tell her little charge frightful stories of ghosts and hobgoblins. If she be allowed, the child's disposition may become timid and wavering, which may continue for the remainder of his life.

Addison* strongly reprobates the custom of telling stories of ghosts to children. "Were I a father," says he, "I should take a particular care to preserve my children from these little horrors of the imagination, which they are apt to contract when they are young, and are not able to shake off when they are in years. I have known a soldier that has entered a breach affrighted at his own shadow, and look pale upon a little scratching at his door, who, the day before, had marched up against a battery of cannon. There are instances of persons who have been terrified even to distraction at the figure of a tree or the shaking of a bulrush. The truth of it is, I look upon a sound imagination as the greatest blessing of life, next to a clear judgment and a good conscience." If a child were not frightened by such stories, darkness would not frighten him more than light. Moreover, the mind, thus filled with fear, acts upon the body, and injures the health. A child should never be placed in a dark cellar, nor frightened by tales of rats, &c. Instances are related of fear, thus induced, impairing the intellect for life.

109.—*Q.* Do you approve of carpets in nurseries?

* "Spectator," No. 12.

A. No; unless it be a small piece for the child to roll upon. Carpets harbour dirt and dust, which is constantly floating about the atmosphere, and thus making it impure for the child to breathe. The truth of this may be easily ascertained by entering a darkened room, where a ray of sunshine is struggling through a crevice in the shutters. If the floor of a nursery must be covered, let oil cloth be used, as this may be washed as often as it is necessary. The less furniture a nursery contains the better, as much furniture obstructs the free circulation of the air.

110.—*Q.* Suppose there is not a fire in the nursery grate, should the chimney be stopped, to prevent a draught in the room?

A. Certainly not. I consider the use of a chimney to be two-fold:—1st. to carry off the smoke; and, 2ndly. (which is of quite as much importance) to carry off the impure air, and thus to ventilate the room.

EXERCISE.

111.—*Q.* Do you approve of sending a child out before breakfast during the summer months?

A. I do, when the weather will permit, and provided the wind be not in an easterly direction; indeed, a child can scarcely be in the open air too much.

112.—*Q.* Should a child be early put on his feet to walk?

A. No: a child should learn to walk himself. He should be put upon a carpet; and it will be found, when he is strong enough, he will hold by a chair and stand alone: when he can do so, and attempts to walk, he may be supported. In the generality of instances, children are put on their feet too soon; and the bones, at that tender age, being very flexible, bend, causing bandy legs.

113.—*Q.* Do you approve of children's carriages?

A. I do not, for two reasons: first, because, when a child is strong enough, he had better walk as much as he will; and, secondly, the motion is not so good, and the muscles are not so much put into action, and consequently cannot be so well developed, as when he is carried.

114.—*Q.* Suppose it be wet under foot, but dry above, do you then approve of sending a child out?

A. If the wind be not in the east, and the air be not damp, let the child be well wrapped up, and sent out. Of course, if he be labouring under an inflammation of the lungs, however slight, or if he be just recovering from one, it would be improper. In the management of children, we must take care neither to coddle nor to expose them unnecessarily, as both are dangerous.

115.—*Q.* How many times a day should a child be sent out in fine weather?

A. Let him be sent out as often as possible. If children lived more in the open air they would not be so susceptible of disease.

116.—*Q.* Suppose it be a wet day what exercise would you then recommend?

A. Let the child run about a large room, or about the hall; and, if it does not rain very violently, put on his hat and throw up the window, taking care he does not stand still while the window is open. Do not any account allow a child to sit any length of time at a table, amusing himself with books, &c.; let him be active and stirring, that his blood may circulate freely, as it ought to do. I would rather see a child actively engaged in mischief than sitting still, doing nothing.

AMUSEMENTS.

117.—*Q.* Have you any remarks to make on the amusements of children?

A. A child should be encouraged to engage in those amusements where the greatest number of muscles are brought into play. For instance, to play at ball or hoop, to run to certain distances and back, and, if it be a girl, to amuse herself with a skipping rope, such being most excellent exercise. A child should never be allowed to have playthings that he may injure himself with; such as toy swords, knives, bows and arrows, &c. I wish to caution you against allowing a boy to ride on a rocking horse. I have known injurious consequences from such an amusement.

EDUCATION.

118.—*Q.* Do you approve of infant-schools?

A. I do, if the arrangements are such that health is considered before learning. Let children be only confined two or three hours a day, and let what little they learn be taught as an amusement rather than as a labour. A play-ground ought to be attached to an infants' school, where, in fine weather, for every half hour they spend in-doors, they should spend one out of doors; and in wet weather they should have, in lieu of the play-ground, a large room to romp and shout and riot in. To develope the different organs, muscles, and other parts of the body, children require fresh air, a free use of their lungs, active exercise, and their bodies to be thrown into all manner of attitudes. Let a child mope in a corner, and he will become stupid and sickly. The march of intellect as it is called, or rather the double-quick march of intellect as it should be called, has stolen a march upon health. Let the march of intellect and the march of health take the same strides, and then we shall have "*mens sana in corpore sano*" (a sound mind in a sound body).

SLEEP.

119.—*Q.* Do you approve of a child sleeping on a feather bed?

A. A feather bed enervates the body, causes rickets, and makes a child crooked. A horse-hair mattress, or a tick stuffed with oat chaff,* is the best for a child to lie on.

120.—*Q.* Do you recommend a child to be put to sleep in the middle of the day?

A. Let a child be put on his mattress awake at twelve o'clock, and let him sleep for an hour or two before dinner, and he will rise refreshed and strengthened for the remainder of the day. I said let him be put down *awake*. He may cry for the first few times, but by perseverance he will fall to sleep without any difficulty. The practice of sleeping before dinner should be continued till the child is two years old, and even longer, if he can be prevailed upon to do so.

121.—*Q.* At what hour should a child be put to bed in the evening?

A. At six o'clock in the winter and seven o'clock in the summer. Great regularity should be observed, as regularity is very conducive to health. As soon as a child can run, he should be encouraged to race

---

* The *oat chaff* may be procured from any farmer, and makes a most excellent bed. It is the chaff of the first winnowing, and requires renewing every year.

about the hall, or a large room, for a quarter of an hour before he goes to bed; which will be the best way of warming his feet, preventing chilblains, and making him sleep soundly.

122.—*Q.* Should a child be washed and dressed *as soon as he awakes* in the morning?

A. If he awake in anything like a reasonable time he should; for if he doses after he has once awoke, such slumber does him more harm than good. He should be up as soon as it is light every morning. If a child is taught to rise early it will make him an early riser for life, and will be likely greatly to prolong his existence.

123.—*Q.* Should a child lie alone?

A. After he is weaned he should do so. He will then rest more comfortably, and his sleep will be more refreshing.

SECOND DENTITION.

124.—*Q.* When does a child begin to cut his second set of teeth?

A. He generally begins to cut them at seven years old. The first set is sometimes cut with a great deal of difficulty, and produces various diseases; the second set is cut without any difficulty, and causes no disease. The following is the process:—One after another of the first set gradually loosen, and either drop out or are pulled out with very little pain or trouble; under which the second or permanent teeth make their appearance, and fill up the vacant spaces. The fang of the tooth that has dropped out is nearly all absorbed or eaten away, leaving little more than the crown. The first set consists of twenty; the second set (including the wise teeth, which are not generally cut till after the age of twenty-one) consists of thirty-two. I would strongly recommend you to pay particular attention to the teeth of your children, as, besides their being so ornamental, their regularity and soundness are of the greatest importance to the present as well as future health of your offspring. If there be any deviation in the appearance of the second set, lose no time in consulting an experienced dentist.

DISEASES, &c.

125.—*Q.* How is a mother to know her child is about to have Water on the Brain, so that she may call in her medical attendant without loss of time?

A. If her child be more than usually excited, if his eye gleams with unusual brilliancy, if his tongue runs faster than it is wont, if his cheek be flushed, and his head be hot, there is cause for suspicion. If to these symptoms be added a more than usual carelessness in tumbling about, in hitching his foot in the carpet, or in dragging one foot after the other; and if, too, he has complained of pains in his head, it may then be known that the first stage of inflammation (the fore-runner of water on the brain) either has taken or is about taking place, and no time should be lost in obtaining medical advice; for now is the golden opportunity, when the child's life may almost to a certainty be saved.

126.—*Q.* When is a mother to know that Croup is about to take place?

A. There is no disease that requires more prompt treatment than croup, and none that creeps on so insidiously. At first the child is troubled with a little dry cough, he is hot and fretful, and he is rather hoarse when he cries; at length *he breathes as though it were through muslin, and the cough becomes crowing.* These two symptoms prove that the disease is now fully formed. If a mother delay to send for assistance, in a few hours it will probably be of no avail, and in a day or two her child may be a corpse.

127.—*Q.* When is a mother to know a cough is not a "tooth cough," but one of the symptoms of Inflammation of the Lungs?

A. If the child's skin be hot and dry, if the lips be parched, or if the *breathing be hurried,* and the appetite be diminished, then there is no doubt inflammation either has taken or is about taking place. No time should be lost in sending for a medical man; indeed, the *hurried breathing* alone should be a sufficient reason for your procuring immediate assistance. If inflammation of the lungs were properly treated at the *onset,* a child would scarcely ever be lost by that disease.

128.—*Q.* If a child has large bowels, what would you recommend likely to reduce their size?

A. It should be borne in mind that the bowels of children are larger in proportion than those of adults. But if they be actually larger than they ought to be, let them be well rubbed night and morning with soap liniment, and let the child be prevented from drinking as much as he has been in the habit of doing.

129.—*Q.* What are the best aperients for children?

A. If it be *actually* necessary to give a child opening medicine, the following will generally answer every purpose:—Take half a drachm of powdered scammony, half a drachm of Turkey rhubarb, two scruples of heavy carbonate of magnesia, three drachms of simple syrup, and nine drachms of aniseed water: mix. Two teaspoonfuls to be given early in the morning occasionally, or, for a change, one or two teaspoonfuls of castor oil may be substituted. Some mothers are in the habit of giving their children jalap gingerbread. I do not approve of it, as jalap is a drastic, griping purgative.

130.—*Q.* When a child is delicate, and his body is gradually wasting away without any assignable cause, and where the stomach rejects all food that is taken, what plan can be adopted likely to support the child's strength, and thus, probably, be the means of saving the child's life?

A. I have seen, in such a case, the greatest benefit to arise from a teacupful of strong mutton broth, used as a glyster, every four hours.

131.—*Q.* If a child be naturally delicate, what plan would you advise to strengthen him?

A. Strict attention to the rules before mentioned, and *change of air*, more especially, if it be possible, near the sea-coast. Change of air sometimes acts like magic upon a delicate child, and restores health where everything else has failed.

132.—*Q.* Do you approve of sea-bathing for young children?

A. No: they are frequently so frightened by it that the alarm does more harm than good. The better plan would be to have the child washed every morning with sea-water, and to have him carried on the beach as much as possible, so that he may inhale the sea-breezes.

133.—*Q.* What is the best method of administering medicine to a child?

A. If he be old enough, appeal to his reason; for if a mother endeavour to deceive her child, and he detect her, he will suspect her for the future.* If he be too young to appeal to his reason, then, if he will not take it, a mother must compel him. Let her lay him across her knee, let his hands and nose be held tightly, and then let the medicine be poured down his throat by means of the patent medicine

* See Abbot's *Mother at Home*, chapter 5th.

spoon, and he will be obliged to swallow it. It may be said that this is a cruel procedure; but it is the only way to compel an unruly child to take medicine, and much less cruel than running the risk of his dying from the medicine not having been administered.

134.—*Q.* Should a sick child be roused from his sleep to give him medicine, when it is time to take it?

A. On no account, as sleep, being a natural restorative, should not be interfered with. A mother cannot be too particular in administering medicine whilst he is awake.

135.—*Q.* Do you not consider that medical men are generally too apt to give larger doses of medicine, or order a greater number of leeches, to a child, from knowing how prone mothers are to administer less medicine, or apply fewer leeches, than have been ordered?

A. Most certainly not. The common practice among some mothers, of disobeying a medical man's orders, or only adopting half his measures, cannot be too strongly reprobated. I will subjoin a few examples. *First Example.*—I will suppose a child five years old to be labouring under a violent inflammation of the lungs, which had existed some days; at length the parents call in their medical attendant. In addition to the medicine he is about to order, he thinks it necessary that six leeches be applied to the chest. He calls in the evening, and finds his little patient no better, nay, worse; he inquires how the leeches bled, and is informed they only put on three leeches, as they were afraid of weakness, and that the child might sink under the loss of blood. The medical man expresses his regret: he considers the child is not now in a fit state to lose more blood, and he considers the only chance of saving the child's life will be to apply a blister. They demur at this, but at length they agree to it's application: the blister is sent. In the mean time one of the neighbours drops in. The blister is mentioned to her; she says she highly disapproves of it, and that, if it were her child, she would not have him so tortured. The parents, too happy in having such advice, as it coincides with their own opinion, are now confirmed in their former determination not to have the blister applied. The medical gentleman calls in the morning, and finds his little patient dying. He asks if the blister had at all risen, and finds, to his chagrin and mortification, that it was not applied! Let me ask, who caused the death of that child? *Second Example.*—A child is in convulsions; the medical attendant is sent for.

On looking into the mouth, he finds the gums very much swollen and very red: he pronounces the convulsions to arise from teething. He then proposes to lance the gums immediately, and to have the child put into a warm bath as soon as warm water can be procured. The mother objects both to the lancing and the warm bath. She says that lancing the gums hardens them, that she will not have the child tormented, and that she has heard of a child who died in a bath. The medical man uses arguments and entreaties; he proves the absurdity of the opinion that lancing the gums hardens them, he brings forward numerous cases where the warm bath has been eminently successful: but all his arguments, all his entreaties, are unavailing. The convulsions continue with redoubled violence, and at length water on the brain is formed. The little patient dies, another victim, out of many, from a medical man's advice not having been attended to. *Third Example.*—A child has had violent inflammation of the lungs. He is very much better, but still there is a vestige of the disease remaining; on which account the medical man recommends the low diet to be continued a little longer. Of course, the child is very weak, and the mother, without consulting the medical man, gives the child broth (which is essence of meat in solution). The broth lights up the dying embers of the inflammation, and the disease returns with redoubled fury; and the child, being now too weak to bear the former remedies, dies! *Fourth Example.*—The last example I shall bring forward is a case of measles. Inflammation of the lining membrane of the lungs constitutes, in most cases, the principal danger in measles. A medical man is called in to such a case. He recommends medicine, that the child should be kept comfortably warm, and that he should live for a few days on barley-water, gruel, and such like simple beverage, and that stimulants, in any shape whatever, should on no account be given. An acquaintance sees the child, and tells the mother that the principal thing to be attended to is, to throw the measles out, and for that purpose she recommends her to give the child tent wine. The wine is given, and what is the consequence? A violent inflammation ensues, which possibly carries the little patient off, when, if the advice of the medical man had been followed, the child (with the blessing of God) would have been still alive! These are all pictures drawn from the life; would that they were but the coinage of the brain! Many more examples might be produced, but these, I hope, will be enough to warn a mother against omitting or adding to any advice which her medical attendant, from experience, might recommend. In short, parents should place the utmost confidence in their professional adviser; for if the utmost confidence does not exist, they have no business to employ him.

136.—*Q.* Have you any remarks to make on the management of a sick room?

A. A sick room cannot be kept too quiet, neither can the air of the apartment be too pure; hence the impropriety of having many in the room, as, if there be many, they cannot help making a noise, and thus they excite the patient; they cannot avoid consuming the oxygen of the atmosphere, and thus they contaminate it. One efficient nurse, or at farthest two, are all that are necessary. A sick room should be kept cool and well-ventilated. Large fires cannot be too strongly condemned; for if there be fever (and there are scarcely any complaints without) large fires only increase it. Small fires encourage ventilation of the apartment, and thus carry off impure air. Of course, if it be summer time, fires would be improper; but still a mother should take care the chimney is not stopped up, as the chimney will carry off the impure air of the room. All evacuations should be removed from the room as soon as passed. If the medical adviser wishes them to be saved, they should be removed to some distant apartment, or to the cellar. Frequent change of linen is quite as necessary, if not more so, during sickness than at any other time. In cases of diseases of the head smelling salts should not be used, as they increase the flow of blood to that part.

137.—Q. Suppose a child to have had inflammation of the lungs, and to be very much predisposed to it, what precautions would you take to prevent it for the future?

A. I would recommend the child to wear fine flannel instead of lawn shirts, to wear good lamb's wool stockings *above the knee*, and to wear constantly a Burgundy pitch plaister (about the size of a tea-saucer) between the shoulder blades, in order to keep the root of the lungs warm. This plaister should not be discontinued till teething be completed, and not even then, if the lungs be still delicate. As soon as one plaister becomes loose, another should immediately take its place. The plaister should be gradually discontinued by cutting off a small piece every morning, to prevent the child from taking cold by its being too suddenly left off. I should also advise table salt or vinegar to be added to the water the child is washed in of a morning, as recommended in answer to the 77th question.

138.—Do you advise such a child to be confined within doors?

A. If there be any inflammation present about the child, or if he has but just recovered from one, it would be improper to send him in the open air, but not otherwise, as the fresh air would be a likely means of strengthening the lungs, and thereby of preventing an attack of inflammation for the future. Besides, the more a child is coddled within doors, the more likely he will be to take cold, and thereby inflammation. If the weather be cold, but not wet nor damp, the child should be sent out, but let him be well clothed; and the nurse should have strict injunctions not to stand about entries or in any draughts, indeed, not to stand at all, but to keep walking all the time she is in the air.

139.—*Q.* If a child be chicken-breasted or narrow-chested, are there any means of expanding and strengthening his chest?

A. Learning should be put out of the question; his health only should be attended to, or consumption will mark him as her own. Let him live in the open air as much as possible, if it be country, so much the better. Let him rise early in the morning, and go to bed betimes; and if he be old enough to use the dumb bells, he should do so daily. Let the child be made to walk, and sit upright, and keep him as much as possible upon a milk* diet ; and let him have fresh meat every day. Stimulants should be carefully avoided. In short, let every means be used to nourish, strengthen, and invigorate the system, without creating fever.

140.—*Q.* If a child wet his bed while asleep, is there any method of preventing him from doing so for the future?

A. Let him be held out just before he himself goes to bed, and again when the family goes to bed. If he be asleep at the time he will become so accustomed to it that he will make water without awaking. He should be made to lie on his side; for if he be put on his back the urine will rest upon an irritable part of the bladder, and if he be inclined to wet his bed he will not be able to avoid doing so. He should not be allowed to drink much with his meals, especially with his supper.

141.—*Q.* Can you tell me of any plan to prevent chilblains, or, if a child be suffering from them, to cure them?

---

* Where milk does not agree, it may be generally made to do so by the addition of a small quantity of lime water.

A. First, then, the way to prevent them:—Let a child who is subject to them wear a square piece of wash leather over the toes, a pair of warm lamb's wool stockings, and good shoes, but above all let him be encouraged to run about the house as much as possible, especially before going to bed. Secondly, the way to cure them:—*If they be unbroken,* let them be well rubbed with opodeldoc night and morning, then covered with a piece of lint, over which let the wash leather be placed. *If they be broken,* let a piece of lint be spread with spermaceti cerate and applied to the part every morning, and a white bread poultice every night.

142.—*Q.* How may worms be prevented from infesting children's bowels?

A. Worms generally infest weak bowels; hence the moment a child becomes strong worms cease to exist. The reason why children are so subject to worms is owing to the very improper food which is generally given to them. When a child is stuffed with fruits, sweets, puddings, and pastry, is there any wonder that he should suffer from worms? The way to prevent them is to avoid such things, and at the same time to give the child plenty of salt to his *fresh* meat.

143.—*Q.* How can a child be prevented from becoming ricketty?

A. By good nourishing diet, by fresh air, and by not allowing the child to bear his weight upon his legs too soon ; by his sleeping on a hard mattress, by ablutions with salt and water, indeed, by strict attention to the rules laid down in these pages ; and, if possible, by change of air to the coast. Whatever is conducive to the general health is preventive of rickets.

WARM BATHS.

144.—*Q.* Have the goodness to mention those complaints of children for which warm baths are useful.

A. 1. Convulsions ; 2. Pains in the bowels, known by the child drawing up his legs, screaming violently, &c. ; 3. Restlessness from teething : 4. Flatulence. The warm bath acts as a fomentation to the stomach and bowels, and gives great ease where the usual remedies do not rapidly relieve.

145.—*Q.* Will you mention the precautions and the rules to be attended to in putting a child into a warm bath?

A. 1. Carefully ascertain, before the child is immersed in the bath, that the water be neither too hot nor too cold. Carelessness, or over-anxiety to put the child in the water as soon as possible, has frequently caused great pain and suffering to the child, from his being immersed in the bath when the heat was too great. Ninety-eight degrees of Fahrenheit is the proper temperature of a warm bath. 2. If it be necessary to add fresh warm water, let the child be either removed the while, or let it not be put in too hot; for if boiling water be added to increase the heat of the bath, it naturally ascends, and may scald the child. Again, let fresh hot water be put in at as great a distance from the child as possible. 3. The usual time for a child to remain in a bath is a quarter of an hour. 4. Let the chest and bowels be rubbed with the hand while the child is in the bath. 5. Let the child be immersed in the bath as high up as the neck, taking care that he be supported under the arm pits, and that his head also be rested. 6. As soon as the child comes out of the bath, he should be carefully rubbed dry, and, if it be necessary to keep up the action on the skin, he should be placed between flannel, or in a blanket; or, if the necessary relief has been obtained, let him be placed between the sheets in his crib, where most likely he will fall into a sweet sleep.

ACCIDENTS.

146.—*Q.* Suppose a child cut his finger, what is the best application?

A. There is nothing better than tying it up with rag in its blood, as nothing is more healing. Do not wash the blood away, but apply the rag at once, taking care, of course, that no foreign substance be left in the wound. If there be glass or dirt in it, it will be necessary to bathe it in warm water, to get rid of it, before the rag is applied. Some mothers apply salt, or Fryar's balsam, or turpentine, to fresh wounds; these plans are all cruel, unnecessary, and even frequently make them difficult to heal. Of course, if it be a severe wound, surgical assistance will be required.

147.—*Q.* If a child receive a blow causing a bruise, what had better be done?

A. Soak a piece of brown paper in one part of French brandy and two of water, and apply it immediately to the part; when dry, renew it. This simple plan will generally prevent swelling or disfiguration. Of course, the above plan would not be proper if it be the parts immediately about the eye that are bruised, as it would cause too much smarting; then, the frequent bathing of the bruise simply with warm water will be as good an application as any other.

148.—Q. If a child's clothes should be on fire, what should be done to extinguish it?

A. Roll him in the rug, carpet, or door mat, or in any thick article of dress you may either have on or have at hand, if it be woollen, so much the better; or roll him over on the floor, as, by excluding the atmospheric air, the flame will go out: hence the importance of a parent cultivating presence of mind. If persons were prepared for such emergencies, such horrid disfigurations and deaths would be less frequent. A parent should have a proper guard before the nursery grate, and should be very strict in not allowing their children to play with fire.

149.—Q. What is the best immediate application to a scald or burn?

A. There is nothing more efficacious than flour. It should be applied very thickly over the part, and kept in its place with rag and a bandage, or tape, or ribbon. If this be done, almost instantaneous relief will be experienced, and the burn or scald will get well quicker than under any other practice. The advantage of flour, as a remedy, is, it always is at hand. I have seen some most extensive burns and scalds cured by the above simple plan. Scraped potatoes, sliced cucumber, salt, cold water, vinegar and water, linseed oil and lime water, spirits of turpentine and corded cotton, have all been recommended; but in my practice nothing has been so efficacious as flour. After the first few days, the burn or scald may, if severe, require different dressings; but if it be severe the child should be placed under the care of a medical man. If the scald be on the leg or foot, a common practice is to take the shoe and stocking off: in this operation the skin is frequently removed also. Now the shoe and stocking should be slit up, and thus taken off; so that no unnecessary pain or mischief may be caused.

PART III.—YOUTH.

ADVICE TO MOTHERS.

PART III.—YOUTH.

ABLUTION.

150.—*Question.* Are you an advocate for cold bathing?

Answer. If the weather be very warm, the water cannot be considered cold, but tepid: such bathing is very beneficial, provided moderation be observed. Many youths bathe every morning in the summer, regardless of the frequent changes of temperature, and remain in the water half an hour each time. Now this practice is most dangerous. Youths should never use cold bathing oftener than every other day, and not so often, unless the weather be very favourable. Nor should they remain in the water longer than five minutes at a time; if they do, instead of being strengthened, they will be weakened by it. Cold bathing does not always agree. Sometimes it arises from persons being quite cold before they plunge into the water. Some have an idea that they should go into the water while their bodies are quite cold. Now this is a most mistaken notion, and likely to produce dangerous consequences. The body should be comfortably warm, but not hot; and then the individual will receive every advantage the cold bathing can produce. If he goes into the bath whilst the body is cold, the blood becomes chilled, and is driven to internal parts, and thus frequently produces mischief. An individual, after using cold bathing, should, if it agree with him, experience a pleasing glow over the whole surface of the body; but if it disagree with him, a chilliness and coldness will be the result, and, in some instances, the lips and nails will become blue. These are proofs that cold bathing is injurious, and therefore should on no account be persevered in, unless these symptoms have hitherto proceeded from his going into the bath whilst he was quite cold. He may warm himself previously to going into the bath by walking briskly for a few minutes.

151.—*Q.* Do you think a tepid* bath may be more safely used?

* A tepid bath from 62° to 96° Fahr.

A. A tepid bath may be used at almost any time, and an individual may remain longer in one with safety, than in a cold bath.

152.—*Q.* Do you approve of warm bathing?

A. Warm bathing* may be used with great advantage occasionally, say once a fortnight. Warm bathing cleanses the skin more effectually than either cold or tepid bathing, but, as it is more relaxing, should not be used so often as either of them. A person should not continue longer than a quarter of an hour in a warm bath.

153.—*Q.* But does not warm bathing, by relaxing the pores of the skin, cause a person to take cold if he exposes himself to the air immediately afterwards?

A. On this point there is a great deal of misconception and unnecessary fear. A person, immediately after using a warm bath, should take proper precautions; that is to say, he should not expose himself to draughts, neither should he wash himself in cold water, nor should he drink cold water immediately after using one. But still he may follow his usual exercise or employment, provided the weather be fine, and the wind be not in the east.

* A warm bath from 97° to 100° Fahr.

CLOTHING.

154.—*Q.* Do you approve of youths wearing flannel next the skin?

A. England is so variable a climate, and the changes from heat to cold, from dryness to moisture of the atmosphere, are so very sudden, that some means are required to guard against their effects. Flannel, as it is a bad conductor of heat, prevents the sudden changes from affecting the body, and thus is a great preservative against cold.

155.—*Q.* Flannel sometimes produces great irritation of the skin: what should be done to prevent it?

A. Persevere in its use, and in a few days the skin will bear it comfortably. The Angola and woven silk waistcoats have been recommended as substitutes, but there is nothing equal to Welch flannel.

156.—*Q.* If a youth has delicate lungs, do you approve of his wearing a prepared hair skin over the chest?

A. I do not. The chest may be kept too warm as well as too cold. The hair skin heats the chest too much, and thereby promotes a violent perspiration, which becomes suddenly checked by cold, and produces mischief. If the chest be delicate, the flannel waistcoat should be made like a double-breasted waistcoat, with a row of buttons on the right and left sides; both sides should be buttoned, thus causing the chest to have a double covering of flannel. A collar similar to that for a night-shirt should be attached to the waistcoat, which will thus keep the throat warm, and be a means of warding off hoarseness and sore throats.

157.—*Q.* Have you any remarks to make on youth's waistcoats?

A. Fashion, in this instance, as in most others, is at direct variance with common-sense. It would seem that fashion was intended to swell the bills of mortality. It might be asked, what part of the chest in particular should be kept warm? The upper part of the chest. It is in the upper part of the lungs that tubercles (consumption) usually first make their appearance; and is it not preposterous to have such parts in particular kept cool? Double-breasted waistcoats cannot be too strongly recommended for men in general, and for youth in particular.

158.—*Q.* Have you any remarks to make on shoes and stockings?

A. The shoes for winter should be thick, and waterproof. If youths be delicate, they should have double soles to their shoes, with a piece of bladder between each sole: this will make them completely waterproof. Youths cannot be too particular in keeping their feet dry, as wet feet are a more frequent source of cold than almost any thing else. If, when they reach home, their feet be at all damp, the shoes and stockings should be immediately changed.

159.—*Q.* When should a girl begin to wear stays?

A. A girl should never wear them.

160.—*Q.* Do not stays strengthen the body?

A. No: on the contrary, they weaken it. *They weaken the muscles.* The pressure upon them causes them to waste; so that in the end girls cannot do without them, as the stays are then obliged to perform the duty of the wasted muscles. *They weaken the lungs* by interfering with their functions. Every inspiration is accompanied by a movement of the ribs. If this movement be interfered with, the function of the lungs is so likewise; and consequently disease is likely to follow, and difficulty of breathing, cough, or consumption, may ensue. *They weaken the heart's action*, and thus oftentimes produce palpitation, and, perhaps, eventually organic or incurable disease of the heart. *They weaken the digestion* by pushing down the stomach and the liver, and by compressing the latter; and thus induce indigestion, flatulence, and liver disease. *They weaken the bowels* by impeding their proper peristaltic motion, and thus produce constipation and ruptures. Is it not presumptuous to imagine that man can improve upon God's works, and that, if more support had been required, the Almighty would not have given it?

161.—Q. But would not a girl grow out of shape if she were not to wear stays?

A. Certainly not; her form would become more natural, and thus more beautiful. Depend upon it, stays, instead of bringing women into shape, frequently have a contrary effect, and make them crooked. Women are more frequently crooked than men; indeed, there are (and facts bear me out in saying so) more crooked women than straight ones. Dr. Forbes, in the *Cyclopædia of Practical Medicine*, states that, in a boarding school containing forty girls, nearly all were more or less crooked. I may here state that female savages are celebrated for their fine figures, and that there is scarcely a crooked one to be found. Let me, then, implore you to be ruled by common sense rather than by fashion. Let the numberless deformed women, and the thousands of patients who have fallen victims to the use of stays, be a warning to you, and deter your daughters, when girls, from wearing them; for remember, if they are worn when young, *they cannot be discontinued afterwards.*

162.—*Q.* Have you any remarks to make on female dress?

A. There is a perfect disregard to health in every thing that appertains to fashion. Parts that should be kept warm are kept cold: the upper part of the chest, most prone to tubercles (consumption), is completely exposed; the feet, great inlets to cold, are covered with thin stockings and shoes, as thin as paper. Parts that should have full play are cramped and hampered: the chest is cribbed in by stays, the feet with tight shoes; hence preventing a free circulation of blood. The mind, that should be calm and unruffled, is kept in a constant state of excitement by balls and routs and plays. The mind and body sympathize with each other, and disease is the consequence. Night is turned into day; and a delicate female leaves the heated ball-room, decked out in her airy finery, to breathe the damp and cold air of night. She goes to bed: for the first few hours she is too much excited to sleep; towards morning, when the air is pure and invigorating, and when to breathe it would be to inhale health and life, she falls into a feverish slumber, and wakes not till noonday. Oh! that parents should be so blinded and infatuated! Can it, then, be wondered at, if the laws of Nature and of common sense be so set at defiance, that one-fourth, and that fourth comprising the most interesting part of the community, that one-fourth of the deaths that occur in Great Britain arise from consumption; that more than fifty thousand die annually of that disease alone?

DIET.

163.—*Q.* Do you consider coffee or tea the most wholesome (where milk does not agree) for a youth's breakfast?

A. Coffee, provided it be made properly. The usual practice of making coffee is, to boil it, to get out the strength! But the fact is, the process of boiling boils the strength away; it drives off that aromatic grateful principle, so wholesome to the stomach, and so exhilarating to the spirit, and in lieu of which extracts its dregs and impurities, which are very heavy, and difficult of digestion. If you wish to have wholesome coffee, you should have a moveable rim of iron attached to the upper part of the coffee pot, on which a muslin bag (which should descend three parts down the coffee pot) should be sewn. The coffee should be placed in this bag, and then boiling water should be poured upon it. It should be allowed to stand for a few minutes, and excellent coffee will be the result.

164.—*Q.* Do you approve of a youth eating meat with his breakfast?

A. This will depend upon the exercise he takes. If he has had a good walk or run before breakfast meat may be taken with advantage, but not otherwise.

165.—*Q.* What is the best dinner for a youth?

A. Fresh mutton or beef. It is a bad practice to allow him to dine on fruit puddings or pastry. Let him be debarred from rich soups and high-seasoned dishes, which only disorder the stomach and inflame the blood. Let him be desired to take plenty of time over his dinner, so that he may be made to chew his food well, and thus that it may be reduced to an impalpable mass, and well mixed with the saliva (which the action of the jaws will cause to be secreted) before it passes into the stomach. If such were the case, the stomach would not have double duty to perform, and youths would not so frequently lay the foundation for indigestion, &c., which may embitter and even make miserable their after life. Greens and trash should not be given. Meat, potatoes, bread, and hunger for their sauce (which exercise will readily give), is the best, and, indeed, should be the only, dinner they should have. Youths should never dine later than two o'clock.

166.—*Q.* Do you consider broths and soups wholesome?

A. The stomach can digest solid food much more readily than liquid, on which account the dinner specified above is far preferable to broths and soups. Fluids in large quantities distend the stomach too much, and hence weaken it, and thus produce indigestion.

167.—*Q.* Do you approve of youths drinking beer with their dinner?

A. There is no objection to a little mild table beer, but strong ale should never be allowed. Indeed, it is questionable whether youths, unless they take unusual exercise, require anything but water with their meals.

168.—*Q.* Do you approve of a youth having a glass of wine after dinner, more especially if he be weakly.

A. I do strongly disapprove of it. His young blood does not want to be set on fire with wine; and if he be delicate I should be very sorry to endeavour to strengthen him by giving him such an inflammable fluid. If he be weakly, he is more predisposed to put on fever, or inflammation of different organs, or consumption; and being thus predisposed, wine would be likely to excite one or other of them into action. A parent should on no account allow a youth to touch spirits, however much diluted; they are still more deadly in their effects than wine.

169.—*Q.* Have you any objection to a youth drinking tea?

A. Not at all, provided it be not green tea, and that it be not made strong. Green tea is apt to make people nervous, and youths *at least* ought not to know what it is to be nervous.

170.—*Q.* Do you object to supper for youths?

A. Meat suppers are highly prejudicial. If they are hungry (and if they have been much in the open air they are almost sure to be so), a piece of bread and cheese, or bread and butter, with a draught of new milk or table beer, will form the best supper they can have. They should not sup later than eight o'clock.

171.—*Q.* Do you approve of youths having anything between meals?

A. I do not; let them have four meals a day, and they will require nothing in the intervals. It is a mistaken notion that "little and often is best." The stomach requires rest as much or perhaps more (for it is frequently very much put upon) than any other part of the body. I do not mean that a boy is to have "*much* and seldom:" moderation is to be observed in every thing. Let him have as much as a growing boy requires (and that is a great deal), but do not let him eat gluttonously, as many indulgent parents encourage their children to do.

172.—*Q.* Have you any objection to a boy having pocket money?

A. It is a bad practice to allow a boy much pocket money; if he is so allowed, he will be loading his stomach with sweet, fruits, and pastry, and thus his stomach will become cloyed and disordered, and the keen appetite so characteristic of youth will be blunted, and ill health will ensue.

EXERCISE.

173.—Q. What is the best exercise for a youth?

A. Walking or running, provided it be not carried to fatigue. The slightest approach to it should warn a youth to desist from carrying it farther.

174.—Q. Do you approve of horse or poney exercise?

A. I do, for a change; but still it should not supersede walking. Horse or poney exercise is very beneficial, and cannot be too strongly recommended. One of the advantages, and the principal one for those living in towns, which it has over walking, is, that a person may go farther into the country, and thus be enabled to breathe a more pure and healthy atmosphere.

175.—Q. Do you approve of carriage exercise?

A. There is no muscular exertion in carriage exercise; the only good it can possibly do is, that it enables a person to breathe a change of air, which may be purer than the one he is in the habit of breathing. But whether it is so or not, change of air frequently does good, even if the air be not so pure. Carriage exercise, therefore, does only partial good.

176.—*Q.* What is the best time of day for taking exercise?

A. In the summer time, early in the morning and before breakfast. If the youth cannot take exercise upon an empty stomach, let him have a slice of bread and a draught of milk. When he returns home, he will be able to do justice to his breakfast. In fine weather he cannot take too much exercise, provided it be not carried to fatigue.

177.—*Q.* What is the best time for him to keep quiet?

A. He should not take exercise immediately after (say half an hour after) a hearty meal, or it will be likely to interfere with digestion.

AMUSEMENTS.

178.—*Q.* What amusements do you recommend for a youth, as being most beneficial to health?

A. Manly games, such as quoits, rackets, ball and skittles. Such games bring the muscles into proper action, and thus cause them to be properly developed. They expand and strengthen the chest; they cause a due circulation of the blood, making it bound merrily through the blood-vessels, and thus diffuse health and happiness in its stream. If games were more patronized in youth, so many miserable nervous creatures would not abound. It would be well if Government would have such places of amusement in every large town ; and if Government would not take it up Public Companies should be formed; and what parent is there that would not lend a helping hand for their support, when his children's health was at stake?

179.—Q. Is playing on the flute, blowing the bugle, or any other wind instrument, injurious to health?

A. Most decidedly so: the lungs and the windpipe are brought into unnatural action by them. Of course, if a youth be of a consumptive habit, this will hold good with tenfold force. If a youth must be musical, let him be taught singing, as that (provided the lungs be not diseased) will be beneficial.

180.—Q. What amusements do you recommend for a girl?

A. Skipping and dancing are among the best. Skipping is exceedingly good exercise for a girl, every part of the body being put into action by it. Dancing, followed as a rational amusement, causes a free circulation of the blood, and is most beneficial, provided it does not induce girls to sit up late at night.

181.—*Q.* If dancing be so beneficial, why are balls such fruitful sources of coughs, colds, and consumptions?

A. On many accounts. They induce young ladies to sit up late at night; they cause them to dress more lightly than they are accustomed to do; and thus lightly clad they leave their homes while the weather is, perhaps, piercing cold, to plunge into a suffocating hot ball-room, made doubly injurious by the immense number of lights, which consume the oxygen intended for the due performance of the healthy function of the lungs. Their partners, the brilliancy of the scene, and the music, excite their nerves to undue, and thus unnatural, action; and what is the consequence? Fatigue, weakness and hysterics, and extreme depression, follow. They leave the heated ball-room at two o'clock in the morning, to breathe the bitter cold, and frequently damp air, of a winter's night; and what is the result? Thousands die of consumption, who might otherwise have lived! Ought there not, then, to be a distinction made between a ball at midnight, and a dance in the evening?

182.—*Q.* But still, would you have a girl brought up to forego the pleasures of a ball?

A. If parents prefer their so-called pleasures to

their health, certainly not; to such mothers I do not address myself.

183.—*Q.* Have you any remarks to make on singing or on reading aloud?

A. Before a mother allows her daughter to take lessons in singing, she should ascertain that there be no actual disease of the lungs, for, if there be, it will probably excite it into action; but if no such disease exist, singing or reading aloud strengthens the chest. Public singers are seldom known to die of consumption.

EDUCATION.

184.—*Q.* Have you any remarks to make on the selection of a female boarding school?

A. Great care should be taken in making choice of one. From twelve to fifteen of a school girl's life comprises the most important epoch of her existence, as regards her future health, and therefore, in a great measure, her future happiness; and one, more than at any other period of her life, when she requires plenty of good nourishment, more especially fresh meat; therefore, ascertain that the pupils have as much good plain wholesome food as they can eat;

ascertain that the school is situated in a healthy spot; that there is a good play-ground attached to it; that the pupils are allowed plenty of exercise in the open air, indeed, that at least one-third of the day is spent there in skipping, gardening, walking, running, &c.; that they are compelled to rise early in the morning, and that they retire to rest early; that each pupil has a separate bed; and that many are not allowed to sleep in the same room, and that the apartments are well ventilated. In fine, their health and their morals should be preferred far before their accomplishments.

CHOICE OF PROFESSION OR TRADE.

185.—*Q.* What profession or trade should you recommend a youth of a delicate or consumptive habit to follow?

A. If a youth be delicate, it is a common practice among parents to put him to some light in-door trade, or, if they can afford it, to one of the learned professions. Such a practice is most absurd, and is fraught with the greatest danger. The close confinement of an in-door trade is highly prejudicial to health. The hard study which is requisite to fit a man to fill the sacred office only increases delicacy of constitution. The stooping at a desk in an attorney's office is most trying to the chest. The harrass, the disturbed nights, the interrupted meals, and the intense study necessary to fit a man for the medical profession, is still more dangerous to health than law, divinity, or any in-door trade. An out-door calling should, therefore, be thought of. If he be respectable, make him a farmer, a tanner, or a land surveyor; but if he be in an inferior station, the trade of a butcher may be recommended. Tanners and butchers are seldom known to die of consumption.

SLEEP.

186.—*Q.* Have you any remarks to make on the sleep of youth?

A. Sleeping rooms are generally the smallest in the house, when, in point of fact, they ought to be the largest. If it be impossible to have a large bed-room, I should advise a parent to have one or two bricks knocked out from over the door of the bed chamber, so as constantly to admit a free current of air from the passages; and in the summer time to have, during the night, the upper window sash lowered about two inches. Fresh air during sleep is indispensable to health; if a bed-room be close, the sleep, instead of being calm and refreshing, is broken and disturbed, and the youth, when he awakes in the morning, feels more tired than when he went to bed. It would be well, if possible, for a youth to have a room to himself; if it be not possible, there should be two beds in the room, as it is much more healthy for a youth to sleep by himself. Bed curtains and valances should on no account be allowed: they prevent a free circulation of the air. A youth should sleep on a horsehair or oat chaff mattress. Such mattresses greatly improve the figure and strengthen the frame. During the day-time, provided it does not rain, the windows should be thrown open; and after a youth has risen from bed he should throw back the bed clothes, that they may become, before the night returns, well ventilated and purified by the air. Plants and flowers should not be allowed to remain in a bedroom at night. Experiments have proved that plants and flowers give off oxygen (a gas so necessary and beneficial to health) in the day-time, and nitrogen (a gas so detrimental, if in larger quantities than it ought to be) in the night-time. Early rising cannot be too strongly insisted upon; nothing is more conducive to health, and thus to long life. Youths are frequently allowed to spend the early part of the morning in bed, breathing the impure

K

atmosphere of a bed-room, when they should be up and out, inhaling the balmy and health-giving fresh breezes of morning. If early rising be commenced early in life it becomes a habit, and will then, probably be continued for the remainder of a man's existence. A youth should on no account be roused from his sleep, but as soon as he is awake in the morning he should be encouraged to rise. Dosing—that state between sleeping and waking—is very injurious; it enervates both body and mind. But if a youth rises early he should go to bed early: it is a bad practice to keep boys up till the family go to bed. A youth should retire to rest by nine o'clock, winter and summer, and rise as soon as he awakes in the morning.

187.—*Q.* How many hours sleep should a youth have?

A. This, of course, will depend upon the exercise he takes; but on an average he should have at least eight hours every night. It is a mistaken notion that youths do better with *little* sleep. Infants, children, and youths, require more sleep than those who are more advanced in years: hence old people can frequently do with very little. This may, in a great measure, be accounted for from the great quantity of exercise the young take, to what the old do. Another reason may be, the young have no pain and no cares to keep them awake, while, on the contrary, the old frequently have one or both.

PREVENTION OF DISEASE, &c.

188.—Q. If a child show great precocity of intellect, is any organ likely to become affected?

A. A greater quantity of arterial blood is sent to the brain of those who are prematurely talented, and hence it becomes more than ordinarily developed. Such advantages are not unmixed with danger: this same arterial blood may excite and feed inflammation; and convulsions, or water on the brain, or insanity, or, at last, idiocy, may follow.

189.—Q. How can danger, in such cases, be warded off?

A. It behoves a parent, if her son be precocious, to restrain him; to send him to a quiet country place, free from the excitement of town; to keep him from books, and, when he is sent to school, to give directions to the master not to tax his intellect too much (for they are too apt, if they have a clever boy, to push him forward); and to keep him from those institutions where a spirit of rivalry is maintained, and the brain thus kept in a state of constant excitement. Medals and prizes are well enough for those who have moderate abilities, but dangerous indeed to those who have brilliant ones. Henry Kirke White was one possessed of precocious talents, and he, alas! fell a victim to them. And, that he may be a warning to parents, I cannot help dilating upon his case. Henry Kirke White died at the age of twenty-one. His biographer, after alluding to his transcendent talents, and at the immense application he made to improve them, goes on to state that " His frame was now totally shaken, and his mind appeared to be worn out. * * * His brother, however, was informed of his danger by a friend, and hastened to Cambridge; but when he arrived he found Henry delirious. The unhappy youth recovered sufficiently to know him for a few moments; the next day he sunk into a state of stupor, and on Sunday, 19th of October, 1806, expired. It was the opinion of his physicians that, if he had lived, his intellect would have been affected." Lord Byron most beautifully speaks of him in the following lines and note :—

"Unhappy WHITE!* when life was in its spring,
And thy young muse just waved her joyous wing,
The spoiler came; and all thy promise fair
Has sought the grave, to sleep for ever there.
Oh! what a noble heart was here undone,
When science' self destroyed her favourite son!
Yes! she too much indulged thy fond pursuit,
She sowed the seeds, but death has reap'd the fruit.
'Twas thine own genius gave the final blow,
And help'd to plant the wound that laid thee low.
So the struck eagle, stretch'd upon the plain,
No more through rolling clouds to soar again,
View'd his own feather on the fatal dart,
And wing'd the shaft that quiver'd in his heart.
Keen were his pangs, but keener far to feel
He nursed the pinion which impell'd the steel;
While the same plumage that had warm'd his nest,
Drank the last life-drop of his bleeding breast."

If Kirke White's brain had not been over-worked (and possibly the emulation of honours may, in a great measure, have been the cause of its being so)

---

* "Henry Kirke White died at Cambridge, in October, 1806, in consequence of too much exertion in the pursuit of studies that would have matured a mind which disease and poverty could not impair, and which death itself destroyed rather than subdued. His poems abound in such beauties as must impress the reader with the liveliest regret that so short a period was allotted to talents which would have dignified even the sacred functions he was destined to assume."—BYRON.

he might still have been alive, a blessing and an ornament to society. If an over-worked precocious brain does not cause the death of the owner, it in too many instances injures the brain irreparably; and the possessor of such an organ, from being one of the most intellectual of children, becomes one of the most stupid of men. The young Roscius, who made such a noise in the world some years ago, and whose brain was over-worked, when he grew up to man's estate, lost that remarkable genius for which his early life had been distinguished. Had his brain been spared when young, when the excitement of youth had worn off (as then there would not have been that danger in study), he might have improved his intellect, and he might now (if he is still living) have possessed talents to have delighted and enraptured mankind.

190.—*Q.* Are precocious youths, in their general health, usually strong or delicate?

A. Delicate. Nature seems to have given a delicate body to compensate the advantages of a talented mind. Precocious individuals are very much predisposed to consumption, perhaps more than to any other disease, with the exception of water on the brain. The hard study which they frequently undergo oftentimes excites the former disease into action.

191.—Q. What habit of body is most predisposed to Scrofula?

A. Those who have a fair, delicate, and almost transparent skin, light eyes, protuberant forehead, rosy cheeks, pouting lips, large joints, and tumid bowels. Of course, the disease is not entirely confined to the above: sometimes those with black hair, dark eyes and complexion, are subject to it, but yet far less frequently than those specified above. It is a remarkable fact that the most talented are the most prone to scrofula; and, being thus clever, their intellects are too often cultivated at the expense of their health. Pulmonary consumption, or mesenteric disease, is frequently their doom. They are like shining meteors; their life is brilliant, but short. Strict attention to the rules of health are the means to prevent scrofula. Sea bathing is most beneficial.

192.—Q. Is a slight spitting of blood to be looked upon as a dangerous symptom?

A. Spitting of blood is always to be looked upon with suspicion, even when the youth appears to be in good health: it is frequently the forerunner of consumption. It may be said that I am alarming a parent unnecessarily by mentioning the fact; but it would be a false kindness if I did not do so. Let me ask, when is consumption to be cured? is it at the onset, or is it when it is confirmed? If parents had been more generally aware that spitting of blood was frequently a forerunner of consumption, they would have taken greater precautions in the management of their offspring; they would have made every thing give way to preserve their health, and they would, in many instances, have been amply repaid by having the lives of their children spared. We frequently hear of patients, in *confirmed* consumption, being sent to Madeira and other foreign parts. Can any thing be more absurd or more cruel? If there be any disease that requires the comforts of home and good nursing more than another, it is consumption.

193.—*Q.* Suppose a youth has spitting of blood, what precautions would you take to prevent it ending in consumption?

A. I would be most particular in his clothing, taking especial care to keep his chest and his feet warm. Let it be winter or summer, if he did not already wear flannel waistcoats, I would recommend him immediately to do so; if it were winter time, I would recommend him also to take to flannel drawers. The feet should be carefully attended to; they should be kept warm and dry, the slightest dampness of either shoes or stockings should cause them to be immediately changed. If a boy, he should wear double-breasted waistcoats; if a girl, high dresses. If it be winter time, he should keep within doors, unless the weather be mild for the season. Particular attention should be paid to the point the wind is in, as he should not be allowed to go out if it be either in the north or east: the latter is more especially dangerous. The diet should be nutritious, but not stimulating. Where milk agrees, there is nothing better for breakfast; indeed, it may frequently be made to agree by the addition of one quarter lime water. Wine and spirits should on no account be allowed. I caution parents in this particular, as many have an idea that wine, in such cases, is strengthening, and that *rum* and milk is a good thing for a cough, or to prevent one. If it be spring and the weather favourable, or summer, or autumn, change of air, more especially to the Welch coast, would be most desirable; indeed, in a case of spitting of blood, I know nothing to be so likely to ward off that formidable and generally intractable complaint, consumption, as change of air. Of course, the beginning of autumn is the best season for visiting the coast. It would be advisable, at the commencement of October, to send him to the south of France, or to a mildpart of England (more especially to Hastings), to winter. But remember, if he be actually in a *confirmed* consumption, I would not recommend you on any account to let him leave his home, as then the comfort of home will far outweigh any benefit of change of air.

194.—Q. Suppose a youth to be very much predisposed to sore throats: what precautions should he take to prevent them?

A. He should bathe his throat externally with lukewarm strong vinegar and water, night and morning. He should also gargle his throat with vinegar and water. He should wear a flannel collar to his flannel waistcoat, as recommended in answer to the 156th question. He should avoid draughts as much as possible; if he be unavoidably in one he should face it. He should take particular care in keeping his feet warm and dry. As he grows up to manhood, he should allow his beard to grow under his throat, as such would be a natural covering for it. I have known the greatest benefit to arise from this simple plan.

195.—Q. You had a great objection to a parent administering calomel to an infant or a child, have you the same objection to her giving it to a youth when he requires opening medicine?

A. Equally as great. It is my firm belief that the frequent use, or rather abuse, of calomel and other preparations of mercury, is oftentimes a source of liver disease and an exciter of scrofula. It is a medicine of great value in some diseases, when given by a judicious medical man; but at the same time it is a drug of great danger when given indiscriminately or too often prescribed. I will grant that in liver diseases it frequently gives temporary relief; but when a patient has once commenced the regular use of it he cannot do without it, till at length the functional ends in organic disease of the liver. The use of calomel predisposes to cold, and thus frequently brings on inflammation and consumption. Family aperient pills should never contain mercury in any form. If a parent wishes to give a youth opening medicine, an agreeable and an effectual one is an electuary composed of best picked Alexandria senna 1oz., best figs 2oz., best raisins 2oz., all chopped very fine. The quantity of a nutmeg may be eaten occasionally, or, for a change, three compound rhubarb pills may be given at bed-time; but, after all, the best opening medicine is attention to diet, exercise, and the other rules of health specified in this little work. If more attention were paid to these points, poor school-boys would not be compelled to swallow such nauseous messes as they usually do. Youths should be desired to visit the water-closet at a certain hour every morning: there is nothing keeps the bowels open so well as establishing this habit.

196.—*Q.* What diseases are female youth most subject to?

A. The diseases peculiar to females are Chlorosis (or Green Sickness) and Hysterics.

197.—*Q.* What are the usual causes of Chlorosis?

A. Chlorosis is caused by torpor and debility of the whole frame, especially of the womb. It is generally produced by scanty or improper food, or by too close application within doors.

198.—*Q.* What are the symptoms of Chlorosis?

A. The patient first of all complains of being languid, tired, and out of spirits. Her complexion gradually assumes a greenish (as Chlorosis signifies) or yellowish hue; there is a dark circle around the eyes; the tongue is generally white and pasty; the appetite is very bad, and frequently depraved. Females labouring under the complaint are sometimes fond of eating chalk, slate pencils, cinder, and sometimes even dirt. They have usually pains on the left side. They suffer greatly from wind, and are frequently nearly choked by it. Their bowels are usually costive, and the stools are depraved. They have generally palpitation of the heart, short dry cough, and are easily out of breath. The legs are frequently swollen. *The menstrual discharge is either entirely suspended or very partially performed.* When the latter is the case, it is usually almost colourless.

199.—Q. How may Chlorosis be prevented?

A. If health were more and fashion less studied, chlorosis would not be such a frequent complaint. This disease generally takes its rise from bad management, from Nature's laws being set at defiance. If young girls had plenty of good wholesome meat, plain roast or boiled (and not stewed, hashed, or highly seasoned) for their stomachs, if they had abundance of good fresh air for their lungs, if they had plenty of good exertion (such as skipping, dancing, running) for their muscles, if their clothing were warm and loose, and adapted to the season, if their minds were kept calm and untroubled from the hurly-burly and excitement of fashionable life, chlorosis would almost be an unknown disease. It is a complaint which country girls know little of; it is a complaint which fine city ladies are too well acquainted with.

200.—Q. What treatment should you advise?

A. The treatment which would prevent it would be the best when it first makes its appearance. If the above means will not remove it, the mother must then apply to her medical adviser, and he will give medicines which will soon have the desired effect. If the disease be allowed to run on for any length of time, it may produce organic disease of the heart, or consumption, or confirmed indigestion.

201.—Q. What are the symptoms of Hysterics?

A. The female is very low-spirited, she is nervous as it is called, she is very much troubled with flatulence; at length the wind rises up towards the throat, giving her the sensation of a ball stopping the breathing, and producing an idea of suffocation. She becomes insensible and apparently faint. After a short time she throws her arms and legs about violently; she laughs boisterously, at other times she makes a peculiar noise; her face is very much distorted; at length she bursts into a flood of tears, and then gradually comes to herself. She may, in a short time, fall into another attack similar to the above.

Hysterics are sometimes frightful to witness, but in themselves are not at all dangerous.

202.—Q. What are the causes of Hysterics?

A. Improper food, excitement of the mind, and want of exercise, are the causes which usually produce hysterics. Hysterics are very frequently feigned, indeed, oftener than any other complaint; and even genuine cases are usually very much aggravated by the patients themselves giving way to them.

203.—Q. What do you recommend an hysterical female to do?

A. To improve her health by proper management, to rise early and take a walk, that she may breathe pure and wholesome air (indeed, she should live nearly half her time in the open air, exercising herself with walking, skipping, &c.); to employ her mind with botany, or any other out-door amusement; to confine herself to plain wholesome food; to eschew fashionable amusements; but above all, not to give way to her feelings, but to arouse herself if she feel an attack approaching. If the fit be upon her, the better plan is for those around to loosen her dress, to dash cold water upon her face, to throw open the window, and then to leave her by herself. If such be done, she will soon come round; but what is the usual practice? If a female be in hysterics, the whole house and perhaps neighbourhood are roused; the room is crowded to suffocation; fears are expressed openly, by those around, that she is in a dangerous state. She hears what they say, and her hysterics are increased ten-fold.

In conclusion, I beg it to be understood that this little work is *exclusively* intended for the perusal of mothers, to guide them in the management of the health of their offspring; to warn them of approaching danger, so that they may promptly apply for medical assistance before illness has gained too firm a footing; to prevent disease where it is possible; to strengthen the delicate; to preserve the health of the healthy; and to make a medical man's task more easy and agreeable by dispelling prejudices, and by proving the importance of strictly adhering to his rules. If I have accomplished any of these points, I am amply repaid for my trouble.

FINIS.